FREEDOM AND JOY

JDV Philosophy Series - 3

FREEDOM AND JOY

Reflections on the Essential Characteristics of Christian Life Today

Kurien Kunnumpuram, SJ
(Professor Emeritus, Jnana-Deepa Vidyapeeth, Pune, India)

Jnana-Deepa Vidyapeeth

&

Christian World Imprints

First Published in 2018 by

Jnana-Deepa Vidyapeeth
Ramwadi, Nagar Road, **Pune-411014**
jdvoffice@jdv.edu.in
www.jdv.edu.in
Phone: +91 20 41036111

&

Christian World Imprints
Christian Publishing & Books from India
H-12 Bali Nagar, **New Delhi-110015**
info@christianworldimprints.com
www.ChristianWorldImprints.com
Phone: +91 11 25465925

ISBN: 978-93-5148-319-9 (HB) ISBN: 978-93-5148-320-5 (PB)

Cataloging in Publication Data--DK
Courtesy: D.K. Agencies (P) Ltd. <docinfo@dkagencies.com>

Kunnumpuram, Kurien, 1931- **author.**
Freedom and joy : reflections on the essential characteristics of Christian life today / Kurien Kunnumpuram, SJ.
pages cm. -- (JDV philosophy series ; 3)
ISBN 9789351483199 (HB)
ISBN 9789351483205 (PB)

1. Christian life. 2. Church history. 3. Francis, Pope, 1936- I. Jnana-Deepa Vidyapeeth, publisher. II. Title. III. Series: JDV philosophy series ; 2.

LCC BV4501.3.K86 2018 | DDC 248.4 23

Printed in India.

CONTENTS

JDV PHILOSOPHY SERIES - 3

Since 1893 Jnana-Deepa Vidyapeeth has been pioneering philosophy discussion and debate inspired by prominent personalities like Richard De Smet, Jean de Marneffe, Salvino Azzopardi, Cyril Desbruslais, Noel Sheth, John Vattanky, etc. It has been in the forefront of promoting Indian philosophy and making philosophical thinking relevant for contemporary times. In its effort to reach out to like-minded scholars, JDV Philosophy Series has been visualized as a catalyst for interdisciplinary thinking and contemporary exploration on social issues fostering holistic liberation, integral development and creative engagement.

JDV Philosophy Series (Books published so far)

1. Salvino Azzopardi: Epistemology and Phenomenology of Religions (2018)
2. Kuruvilla Pandikattu & Thomas Karimundackal (ed): Melodies from the Flute (2018)
3. Kurien Kunnumpuram: Freedom and Joy (2018)

INTRODUCTION

Collected in this book are sixteen articles written at different times and for different purposes. Some of them were published in the *Asian Journal of Religious Studies* while the others were written specifically for this book.

The articles are divided into two parts. Part One deals with different dimensions of Christian existence today. Part Two contains reflections on four recent documents from Rome.

I have been a teacher of theology for about 50 years. The insights I gained during these years into the various dimensions of Christian life today are articulated in the first twelve articles of the book. The next three articles reflect on the three inspiring letters of Pope Francis. The last paper is a discussion of a recent document on the formation of priests issued by the Congregation of the Clergy.

I wish to express my grateful thanks to all who helped me in the writing of this book. Special thanks are due to Fr. P T Mathew, SJ, for his excellent editorial assistance and to Mrs. Gracy P. V. for her competent secretarial help.

Kurien Kunnumpuram, SJ
Kozhikode
10 Sept 2018

I am sorry to inform you that this may be the last book of Rev Kurien Kunnumpuram SJ. Currently he is recuperating at Kozhikode, Kerala, from an operation he had for clot in the brain. He is in a critical state. But let us hope and pray that he will come out of this crisis.

Kuruvilla Pandikattu
General Editor

PART ONE

DIMENSIONS OF CHRISTIAN EXISTENCE TODAY

1

THE CHURCH OF JESUS' DREAMS

1. Preliminary Remarks

1) Unfortunately, Jesus did not write a book to describe the Church of his dreams. But he articulated it in his preaching and teaching. And this articulation has come down to us in the gospels.
2) But the gospels were written several decades after the death of Jesus. The Gospel of Mark was most likely written in the sixties of the first century; Matthew in the late 80's; Luke in early 80's and John in the late 90's.
3) How was the story of Jesus and his teaching preserved during the intervening years? They were remembered and handed on by the disciples of Jesus. Now memory involves two things. 1. Selection. It was not possible for the disciples to remember all that Jesus said and did. They chose to remember and hand over to others what, they thought, would be beneficial to them. 2. Adaptation. They orally communicated to others the message of Jesus in the way that they could understand and accept.

But a third thing happened: Translation. Jesus spoke in Aramaic. But the gospels were written in Greek.

As a result of this two things can be said:

1. The Gospels primarily depict the life and faith of the early Church.
2. By applying certain criteria which Scripture scholars have formulated - like multiple attestation – we can find the authentic words of Jesus with some certainty.

These preliminary remarks must be kept in mind by those who read the rest of the article.

2. The Children of God

The members of the Church are called to be the disciples of Jesus Christ. And the disciples of Jesus are the children of God.

All the four Gospels speak of God as Father – Matthew 44 times; Mark 4 times; Luke 17 times; and John 109 times. "However Matthew exceeds the other evangelists in presenting God as the Father of the disciples. Out of fifty references to God as the Father of human beings in the NT, twenty – one are in Matthew.. In all these twenty-one times God is referred to specifically as the Father of the disciples."[1]

After a thorough investigation of the theme – God as the Father of the disciples – Henry Pattarumadathil has come to the conclusion:

> The Father-children relationship is reserved as a privilege of those who follow Jesus. So Jesus speaks about the Father only to them. His frequent reference to God as the Father of the disciples shows that Jesus is treating his disciples as the children of the Father."[2]

In this connection I wish to print out that there is a problem here. Does Jesus in Matthew consider his disciples to be already children of God or is it a status they are yet to attain? In answer to this question H. Pattarumadathil asserts:

> By responding affirmatively to the call of Jesus the disciples have received the grace to become the children of the Father. But it is their way of life in this world that will be the decisive criterion by which they will be judged as children or as non-children. Therefore, it is not an already attained status but a future state which will be given at the end of the process which has been already initiated.

I have some difficulty in accepting this position. My reasons are the following:

1) Jesus does not at all say that the disciples will be the children of God, if they fulfil certain conditions. He just calls them children of God.
2) In the Christian scheme of things, the moral action of a believer follows from his new being. According to Paul those who believe and are baptized have put on Christ. Or if anyone is in Christ, there is a new creation (2 Cor 5:17). The moral behaviour of a believer is the consequence of his being a new creation. As Paul exhorts the Romans: "Therefore, we have been buried with him through baptism into death in order that, just as Christ was raised from the dead through the glory of the Father, we too might walk in newness of life" (Rom 6:4). "For salvation is nearer to us now than when we became believers; the night is far gone, the day is near. Let us then lay aside the works of darkness and put on the armor of light; let us live honorably as in the day, not in revelling and drunkenness, not in debauchery and

> licentiousness, not in quarreling and jealousy. Instead, put on the Lord Jesus Christ, and make no provision for the flesh" (Rom 13:11-14).

Paul reminds the Ephesians:

> Once you were darkness, but now in the Lord you are light. Live as children of light – for the fruit of the light is found in all that is good and right and true. (Eph 5: 8-9)

3) Christians are already children of God, but it is through their good deeds that they will fully realize their vocation to be children of God.

3. Brothers and Sisters

Since all the members of the Church are children of God, they are brothers and sisters of one another. In the Sermon of the Mount Jesus speaks of the disciples as brothers and sisters at least five times: "If you are angry with a brother or sister you will be subject to judgment. Again, anyone who says to a brother or sister, 'Raca,' is answerable to the court. And anyone who says, 'You fool!' will be in danger of the fire of hell. "Therefore, if you are offering your gift at the altar and there remember that your brother or sister has something against you, leave your gift there in front of the altar. First go and be reconciled to them; then come and offer your gift. (Matt 5:22-24). Again: "And if you greet only your brothers and sisters, what more are you doing than others". (Matt 5:47).

Jesus stood for radical equality among his disciples precisely because they are brothers and sisters. In fact, he forbids even the assumption of titles that suggest a denial of the basic equality of all the members of the Church: "But you are not to be called rabbi, for you have one teacher and you are all students. And call no one your father on earth, for you have one Father – the one in heaven. Nor are you to be called instructors, for you have one instructor, the Messiah" (Matt 23: 8-10).

The early Church was quite aware that all Christians are brothers and sisters. In fact the first Christians called each other brother or sister. And this practice is taken up in the Letters of the New Testament. See The Letter of James 1:2; The First Letter of Peter 2:17; The First Letter of John 2:9-10; 4:20; The Letter of Paul to the Romans 1:13; 16:17; The First Letter of Paul to the Coronthians 1:10.

Jesus' idea of the radical equality of all the members of the Church finds echoes among the early Christians. Thus, Paul writes to the Galatians: "There is no longer Jew or Greek, there is no longer slave or free, there is no longer male and female; for all of you are one in Christ Jesus.

In this context it is instructive to recall the words of Rosemary Radford Ruether. She holds that, in the Christianity reflected in the Gospels and in Paul, "the Church functioned as a counter-cultural community which claimed priority in the lives of its members and dissolved the primacy of one's commitment to the family." She goes on to add:

Christians departed from the natural family and voluntarily joined a new community which was fraternal, equal, without social hierarchies or master-slave relations. There were widespread experiments at communal living. A new family, a new humanity, defined by Christ, was emerging. Christanity, appealing to individuals and to personal responsibility, disrupted the socio-religious ties in the old family structure. To depart from the family religion was to depart from the religion of the ancestors and of the nation. This was subversion, amounting to treason. To follow Christanity was, in the eyes of many, "to strike at the heart of the social order of both the family and the State." There was a political dimension to it. Thus, early Christianity easily invited persecution.[3]

4. Lifestyle

Jesus clearly outlined the way his followers – the members of his Church – are expected to live.

4.1 Righteousness

Jesus demands that his disciples practise righteousness (Matt 6:1). This demand is expressed in different ways : "Fulfil all righteousness" (3:15); "hunger and thirst for righteousness" (5:6); "persecuted for righteousness' sake" (5:10); "Unless your righteousness exceeds" (5:20); "perform righteous deeds" (6:1); "God's Kingdom and his righteousness (6:33); "in the way of righteousness" (21:32): If we read these texts together with Matthew 7:21-28 (which is the conclusion of the Sermon on the Mount), we will get a clear idea of the meaning of righteousness. In 7:21 Jesus points out the necessity of doing the will of the Father for entering the Kingdom. In 7:22-23, Jesus tells the audience that it is not enough to listen to his words, but it is absolutely necessary to put them into practice. As has been pointed out:

> The three expressions "to do righteousness", "to do the will of my Father" and "to do my words" designate the same human action which is necessary for entering into the kingdom of heaven. They express three essential aspects of the conduct of an authentic disciple: he /she should live according to the right norms (practising righteousness), which are determined by the Father (doing the will of the Father) and communicated authoritatively by Jesus (acting in accordance with Jesus' words).[4]

4.2 Love

Jesus clearly states that loving others is fundamental to the discipleship of Jesus. "By this everyone will know that you are my disciples, if you have love for one another" (Jn 13:35). In chapter fifteen of John this is further clarified. "As the Father has loved me, so I love you... This is my commandment that you love one another as I have loved you" (Jn 15:9, 12). The love that comes to us from the Father through Christ should be spread abroad. Our response to God's offer of love in Jesus Christ is not to love God or Jesus but to love our fellow human beings.

In the Sermon on the Mount Jesus asks us to do something more: "But I say to you, Love your enemies and pray for those who persecute you so that you may be children of your Father in heaven; for he makes his sun rise on the evil and on the good, and sends his rain on the righteous and on the unrighteous" (Matt 5:44-45). In other words, as children of the Father who loves people unconditionally we have to love others, including our enemies.

4.3 Trust

Jesus exhorts the disciples and through them all the members of the Church to place all their trust in the Father:

> Therefore I tell you, do not worry about your life, what you will eat or what you will drink, or about your body, what you will wear. Is not life more than food and the body more than clothing? Look at the birds of the air; they neither sow nor reap nor gather into barns, and yet your heavenly Father feeds them. Are you not of more value than they? And can any of you by worrying add a single hour to your span of life? And why do you worry about clothing? Consider the lilies of the field, how they grow; they neither toil nor spin, yet I tell you, even Solomon in all his glory was not clothed like one of these. But if God so clothes the grass of the field, which is alive today and tomorrow is thrown into the oven, will he not much more clothe you-you of little faith? Therefore do not worry, saying, 'What will we eat? Or What will we drink? or 'What will we wear? For it is the Gentiles who strive for all these things. But strive first for the kingdom of God and his righteousness, and all these things will be given to you as well. (Matt 6:25-34).

In this text three things are noticeable:

1) Jesus asks the disciples not to be anxious by pointing out the causes of their anxiety." It is the result of their wrong perspective on life. "Is not life more than food and the body more than clothing"? If God freely gives life and body as gifts, why should they be worried about little things like food and clothing. 2). A second reason for their worry is their lack of awareness of their own limitations. "And which of you by being anxious can add one hour to for his span of life". 3) The third reason for their anxiety is their little faith". "But if God so clothes the grass of the field....will he not much more clothe you, O men of little faith."[5]

2) The assurance of the Father's Care
Jesus tells the disciples that "Your heavenly Father knows that you need all those things". And he assures them that they are more precious to their Father than the birds of the air which he feeds and the lilies of the field which he clothes.

3) Right priority

Jesus asks the disciples to have the right priority in their lives. Instead of worrying about food and clothes they must seek the Kingdom of God and his righteousness. The Greek expression used here implies certain exclusivity. Hence, they must only seek the Kingdom and all these things will be given to you as well. Here let me quote H. Pattarumadathil who observes:

> As seen in the previous chapter, "Kingdom" refers to the dominion and sovereignty of God over his people. So seeking his kingdom would mean seeking God himself as the lord and supreme ruler of their life. At the same time, the kingdom is the end stage of their process. Hence seeking the kingdom would also mean seeking things or living a life that will lead them to the kingdom.

4.4 Forgiveness

In the prayer "Our Father" which Jesus taught the disciples there is a petition "And forgive our debts as we have forgiven our debtors" (Matt 6:12). Here, God is asked to forgive us just as we have forgiven our debtors. This is a comparison. At the end of the Our Father Jesus makes two powerful statements: "For if you forgive others their trespasses, your heavenly Father will also forgive you; but if you do not forgive others, neither will your Father forgive your trespasses". (Matt 6: 14-15).

But this seems to go against the general thrust of Christian faith and Christian life. In chapter 18 of Matthew's Gospel we have the Parable of the Unforgiving Servant. (Matt 18:23-24). In this parable the king forgave the debts of one of his slaves because he pleaded for mercy. But this slave refused to forgive a fellow slave who owed him a very small amount. Now the king tells him: "Should you not have had mercy on your fellow slave, as I had mercy on you" (18:33). This reveals the structure of Christian life: God has loved you, so you must love others. Again, God has forgiven you, so you must forgive others. St Paul understood Jesus' mind on forgiveness. That is why he tells the Colossians: "Just as the Lord has forgiven you, so you must also forgive" (Col 3:13).

4.5 Avoid Ostentation

Jesus asks his disciples, and so the members of his Church, not to perform their righteous actions, in order to be seen and appreciated by other people. He also condemns the ostentatious practices of the hyprocrites who make a show of their pious actions. Jesus does not clarify who the hypocrite is. But the root meaning of hypocrite is an actor. So, what Jesus is asking the disciples is that their pious practices should not be play - acting.

Jesus gives three examples of honest piety:

1) "But when you give alms, do not let your left hand know what your right hand is doing so that your alms may be done in secret; and your Father who sees in secret will reward you" (Matt 6:3-4).
2) "But whenever you pray, go into your room and shut the door and pray to your Father in secret; and your Father who sees in secret will reward you" (Matt 6:6).
3) "But when you fast, put oil on your head and wash your face, so that your fasting may be seen not by others but by your Father who is in secret and your Father who sees in secret will reward you" (Matt 6: 17-18).

What does Jesus mean by the statement: your Father sees your pious practices done in secret and will reward you? This is how H. Pattarumadathil explains it:

Jesus repeatedly assures the disciples that their Father sees their actions performed in secret and that he will reward them (6, 4.6.18). It may be easier to believe in a revealing or manifesting God than to believe in an invisible God. Only a person with deep faith can experience the presence of a God who is in secret (6, 4.6.18) and feel confident of the Father's seeing one's good works done in secret. The assurance of the Father's seeing their good works in secret invites the disciples to go beyond their limited sense experiences and grow in that faith which demands an absolute trust in their Father who is omniscient and omnipotent. It is the same trust and confidence that would strengthen the disciples to face persecutions and trials fearlessly (5:10-12; 10; 18-20.29-31).[6]

It is obvious that Jesus' exhortation to avoid all ostentation applies not only to these practices – alms-giving, praying and fasting- but to the totality of our Christian life.

4.6 Come to the Aid of the Poor and the Needy

In the well-known description of the Last Judgement (Matthew 25:31-46) Jesus asks his followers to go out to those who are poor, hungry, sick or inprison and render them whatever assistance they can. Jesus looks upon the aid given to the needy people as aid given to him: "Truly I tell you, just as you did it to one of the least of my brothers or sisters you did it to me" (Matt 25:40).

The description of the Judgement makes it abundantly clear to me that the only criterion by which my life is judged as a success or a failure in the eyes of Jesus Christ is this: Whether or not I have loved and served people in need.

4.7 Do not Judge Others (Lk 6:37)

Notice that Jesus does not ask us: Do not judge others harshly, but simply: do not judge others. There is a good reason for this command of Jesus: We are not competent to judge others. In order to judge a person I must know his/her family background, his/her educational level, his/ her outlook on life, the pressures under which he/she lives, the temptations he/she is exposed to, and so on, But I do not know most of these things. Hence, I am not competent to judge others. To judge others is not only unchristian but also stupid.

The best thing to do is to leave all judgement to God who can read the hearts and minds of people.

We have to make a distinction between judging a person and evaluating the external behaviour of a person. If you are a teacher, a superior or a formator, you have the right and the duty to evaluate the external behaviour of people who are in your charge.

5. Worship

In this section I shall deal with two topics: 1. The Eucharist; 2. Prayer

1) The Eucharist

I am inclined to believe that the Eucharist refers to three events in the life of Jesus. First of all, it points to Jesus' death on the cross. St Paul was the first New Testament author to affirm this: "For as often as you eat this bread and drink the cup, you proclaim the Lord's death until he comes" (1 Cor 11:26). The Synoptics too allude to this when they speak of "my blood of the covenant which is poured out for many for the forgiveness of sins" (Matt 26:28; see also Mk 14:22; Lk 20:22). As a result, the Church has always looked upon the Eucharist as the sacramental enactment of the sacrifice of Calvary. As Vatican II succinctly expresses it: "Through the hands of priests and in the name of the whole Church, the Lord's sacrifice is offered in the Eucharist in an unbloody and sacramental manner until He Himself returns."

Now what is the meaning of death of Jesus? As Paul points out, Jesus "was handed over to death for our trespasses and was raised up for our justification" (Rom 4:25). In other words, God offers his forgiving love to sinful humans through the death and resurrection of Jesus Christ. And the Eucharistic celebration is the renewal of this offer of forgiving love. Our response to this offer is faith. Hence it is with deep faith in God's forgiving love that we should participate in the Eucharistic celebration.

But there is another way of looking at Jesus' death. For death is the culmination of Jesus' total self-surrender to God in obedience. According to Paul, Jesus "became obedient to the point of death – even death on cross" (Phil 2:8; see also Rom 5:19; Heb 5:8-9). Consequently, the Eucharistic celebration invites all the faithful to surrender themselves totally to God. Vatican II asks priests "to instruct them to offer to God the Father the divine victim in the sacrifice of the Mass and to join to it offering of their own lives."

Secondly, the Eucharist refers to the Last Supper. The death (and resurrection) of Jesus Christ could be celebrated in a variety of ways. That it is now celebrated in the form of a community meal is because of the Last Supper. As Vatican II has taught:

> At the last supper, on the night when He was betrayed, our Saviour instituted the Eucharistic Sacrifice of His Body and Blood. He did this in order to perpetuate the sacrifice of the Cross throughout the centuries until He should come again and so to entrust to His beloved spouse, the Church, a memorial of His death and resurrection.

Hence, the Eucharist is the family meal of the Christians. This demands of us that we participate in it with brotherly/sisterly love. With anger or hatred in our hearts we cannot meaningfully celebrate the Eucharist. The words of the Lord are quite relevant here: "So when you are offering your gift at the altar, if you remember that your brother or sister has something against you, leave your gift there before the altar and go; first be reconciled to your brother or sister and then come and offer the gift" (Matt 5:23-24).

Thirdly, the Eucharist refers to Jesus' table-fellowship with 'tax collectors and sinners'. As George Soares-Prabhu has pointed out:

> It is quite certain, then, that Jesus did habitually dine with the religious and social outcasts of his society, even though this behaviour of his aroused sharp and sustained criticism from the religious elite. References to such table-fellowship are found in all the commonly recognized strands of the Synoptic tradition, in MK (2:16-17), in Q (Mt 11:16-19 = Lk 7:31-35) and in the special material of Luke (15:1ff) and Matthew (21:31ff).[7]

It was quite natural for the disciples of Jesus to have communal Eucharistic meals in order to remember him after his death and resurrection, since such meals were an important part of his life and ministry. Now what did such table-fellowship signify? According to Norman Perrin:

> The central feature of the message of Jesus is, then, the challenge of the forgiveness of sins and the offer of the possibility of a new kind of relationship with God and with one's fellow humans. This was symbolized by a table-fellowship of such joy and gladness that it survived the crucifixion and provided the focal point for the community life of the earliest Christians, and was the most direct link between that community life and the pre-Easter fellowship of Jesus and his disciples.[8]

Hence, Jesus' table-fellowship has a salvific significance. "The inclusion of sinners in the community of salvation, achieved in table-fellowship, is the most meaningful expression of the message of the redeeming love of God."[9] The table-fellowship points to the nature and scope of this love. As Soares-Prabhu remarks:

> Through his table-fellowship with the social and religious outcasts Jesus thus demonstrates in a most convincing way that God's love is not conditional, not restricted to the religious elite who would like to monopolize it, but reaches out without exception to all. There are no outcasts for God.[10]

This has implications for our Eucharistic celebration. It must be an open celebration where the poor, the marginalized, the Dalits and the outcasts are warmly welcomed and their human dignity is powerfully affirmed. They must also be treated as equal members of the community of salvation.

2. Prayer

There are four things which Jesus says about prayer.

1) Avoid verbosity in prayer.

"When you are praying do not heap up empty phrases as the Gentiles do; for they think that they will be heard because of their many words. Do not be like them, for your Father knows what you need before you ask him" (Matt 6: 7-8).

2) Pray with confidence – Jesus asks his disciples to have the trust that their heavenly Father will hear their prayer:

> So I say to you: Ask and it will be given to you; seek and you will find; knock and the door will be opened to you. For everyone who asks receives; the one who seeks finds; and to the one who knocks, the door will be opened. "Which of you fathers, if your son asks for a fish, will give him a snake instead? Or if he asks for an egg, will give him a scorpion? If you then, though you are evil, know how to give good gifts to your children, how much more will your Father in heaven give the Holy Spirit to those who ask him!" (Lk 11:9-13)

There is a hint here that the disciples should pray not so much for material blessings, but for the gift of the Holy spirit.

3) Persevere in prayer

And he said to them, suppose one of you has a friend, and you go to him at midnight, and say to him, 'Friend, lend me three loaves of bread; for a friend of mine has arrived, and I have nothing to set before him. And he answers from within, 'Do not bother me; the door has already been locked, and my children are with me in bed; I cannot get up and give you anything. I tell you, even though he will not get up and give him anything because he is his friend, at least because of his persistence he will get up and give him whatever he needs. (Lk 11:5-8)

4) Pray in this way:

> Our Father in heaven, hallowed be your name, your kingdom come, your will be done, on earth as it is in heaven. Give us today our daily bread. And forgive us our debts, as we also have forgiven our debtors. And lead us not into temptation but deliver us from the evil one (Matt 6: 9-13).

We are so familiar with this prayer that it fails to make any deep impression on us. Father Samuel Rayan says that this is a "subversive prayer". He has made some thought provoking reflections it:

> The kingdom of God should come on earth, and the will of God must be done on earth and thus the name of God must be experienced as meaningful on earth. This is the basic concern; the three statements mean practically the same thing, The first part of the Our Father is a version of an old Jewish prayer. What Jesus adds to this prayer to make it concrete and pointed and give it teeth to bite into the texture of human history, is the second part. God's name is experienced as meaningful and his reign keeps coming when everybody who is hungry has bread to eat, when everybody who needs forgiveness and acceptance is already forgiven and bread is made abundant. It is our task to make both bread and forgiveness, symbols of the new community, available to everybody. The Lord's prayer is, therefore, not merely a good model prayer; it is above all a programme of action, which is very concrete, and has to do with the acceptance of people and bread for the breadless, security for the threatened and honour for the dishonoured. To say the Our Father is to commit ourselves to such action. To live the prayer actively is to become the Church.

6. Leadership

Jesus makes a powerful statement on the kind of leadership that is acceptable to him:

> You know that those who are regarded as rulers of the Gentiles lord it over them, and their high officials exercise authority over them. Not so with you. Instead, whoever wants to become great among you must be your servant, and whoever wants to be first must be slave of all. For even the Son of Man did not come to be served, but to serve, and to give his life as a ransom for many. (Mk 10:42-45).

Jesus makes it abundantly clear that there is no place among his followers, that is in his Church, for the kind of "lording it" over that takes place in the secular world: "it shall not be so among you (Mk 10:41; see also Matt 20:24-28).

He seems to say that the leaders of the Church should follow his example. "The Son of Man came not to be served but to serve" (Mk 10:45).

If we accept Jesus as a model for the leaders of the Church there are three important dimensions we have to pay attention to:

1) A Christian leader has to be a life-giving and growth promoting person. Jesus declared: "I came that they may have life, and have it abundantly" (Jn 10:10)
2) A Christian leader must be ready to render humble, lowly service – After washing the feet of the disciples Jesus told them: "For I have set you an example, that you also should do as I have done" (Jn 13:15)
3) A Christian leader must be prepared to lay down his/her lives for the welfare of others. Jesus asserts: "I am the good shepherd. The good shepherd lays down for his sheep" (Jn 10:11)

   Two things are remarkable in the New Testament: 1. All the leaders of the Church are called ministers. Diakonia is the core of every ministry. Jesus, the servant, is the pattern for all ministers in the Church.

   2. It is highly significant that the New Testament avoids using any of those words (like *Arche, Time, Telcos*) for the ministers the Church which in secular Greek were applied to civil and religious authorities.

   But in course of time a hierarchical conception of authority developed in the Church. The term hierarchy (sacred authority) was invented by a Syrian monk, Psuedo-Dionysius the Areopagite, about 500 A. D. He had a grandiose vision of an ordered universe with everything in its proper level, related to levels above and levels below. His vision comprised a heavenly hierarchy, an earthly hierarchy and an ecclesiastical hierarchy. Because it was mistakenly thought that this Dionysius was a disciple of St Paul, his ideas were easily accepted.

However, in our day`there are some signs that the Church will recapture the spirit of Jesus. In the Dogmatic Constitution on the Church Vatican II clearly stated: The ministers of the Church are servants of their brothers and sisters; their service consists in this that they coordinate the activities of all and direct them toward a common goal – salvation – while respecting their God – given dignity and freedom.[11]

In 1998 Pope John Paul II, while speaking about the ministry of the Pope, affirmed: This service of unity, rooted in the action of divine mercy, is entrusted within the college of bishops to one among those who have received from the Spirit the task, not of exercising power over the people – as rulers of the Gentiles and their great men do (cf Mt 20:25; Mk 10:42)-but of leading them toward peaceful pastures.[12]

If all those entrusted with the ministry of leadership in the Church will take to heart the words of the late Pope, then we will witness the emergence of a new kind of Church leaders.

By way of conclusion I would like to say this: Jesus challenges all the members of the Church to strive earnestly to make our Church ever more truly the Church of his dreams.

Notes

1. H. Pattarumadthil, *Your Father in Heaven: Discipleshipin Matthew as a Process of Becoming Children of God,* Rome : Editrice Instituto Biblico, 2008, p. 29.
2. R.R. Ruether, "Church and Family in Scripture and in Early Christianity" in *New Blackfriars,* and Vol. 654, no 763 (January 1984), p. 6.
3. *Ibid.* pp. 7-8
4. H. Pattarumadathil, *Your Father in Heaven....*p. 35.
5. See H. Pattarumadathil, *Your Father in Heaven,* pp. 114 to 125.
6. *Ibid.* p. 123.
7. *See 1 on p.* 187 G. Soares-Prabhu, "The Table Fellowship of Jesus: Its Significance for Dalit Christians in India Today", in I. Padinjarekuttu, (ed.) *Collected Writings of George M. Soares-Prabhu,* vol. 1, Pune: Jnana-Deepa Vidyapeeth, 1999, p. 225.
8. *See 3 p.* 188 N. Perrin, *Rediscovering the Teaching of Jesus,* London: SCM Press, 1967, p. 107.
9. *See n.* 5 p. 188 G. Soares-Prabhu, *"The Table Fellowship of Jesus",* pp. 233-234.
10. S. Rayan, "The Church – The Jesus' Movement" in K. Kunnumpuram, (ed.) *Collected Writings of Samuel Rayan,* Vol.1. Delhi: ISPCK, 2013, p. 187.
11. Vatican II, Dogmatic Constitution on the Church, Rome, 1964, n. 18.
12. John Paul II, *Ut Unum Sint,* Rome, 1995, n. 94.

2

THE LEADERSHIP STYLE OF POPE FRANCIS

Introduction

In 2014, Chris Lowney published a book on the leadership style of Pope Francis.[1] In it he points out that the Pope did not receive any special training to lead the Catholic Church as Pope. The training he got was to be a Jesuit. Lowney contends that his Jesuit training has a huge impact on the way Pope Francis leads the Church.[2] "His Jesuit background has informed his leadership values and principles."[3] As the Pope confesses: "I feel like I am a Jesuit in terms of my spirituality, what I have in my...heart... Also, I think like a Jesuit."[4]

Jesuit spirituality can be understood only in the context of Ignatius' vision of the religious life in the Society of Jesus. As Lowney points out:

> The Jesuit founder envisioned a religious order plunged into the world, not sheltered in monasteries. Hence, he had to develop practices conductive to success amid the chaotic, distracting, tempting, confusing busyness that characterizes the work world. No wonder, then, that Ignatius' ideas are useful not only to Jesuits but to the rest of us as well, whatever our religious beliefs may be.[5]

The Spiritual Exercises of St Ignatius plays a crucial role in the spiritual formation of the Jesuits. Jesuit novices make these exercises for 30 continuous days. During these days they meditate on the life of Jesus, their personal life history and the way in which they have to follow Jesus.

Pope Francis made these exercises at least twice: once as a novice and a second time as a tertian. For several years, as Novice Master, he guided the month's retreat of his novices. So it is quite certain that his spirituality is well grounded in the Spiritual Exercises of St Ignatius. His life and activities as Pope bear witness to it.

Some of the elements in the training of the novices are uniquely Jesuit. For example, Ignatius prescribed that each novice spend "a month in making a pilgrimage without money, but begging from door to door at times…in order to grow accustomed to discomfort in food and lodging." Ignatius wanted to shake the trainees free from their reliance on "money or other created things" and spur them to rely on God alone. The pilgrimage helped to develop that attitude.[6] Besides, Ignatius wanted "tough, resilient Jesuits who could struggle through discomfort and overcome adversity". It is very likely that the idea of a pilgrimage has had a great impact on Pope Francis, for he "repeatedly uses the metaphor of life as a journey."[7] In fact, he would like to see a Church which is on a pilgrimage.

There are other aspects of Jesuit formation and Jesuit practices that exerted a lot of influence on this Jesuit Pope, but we shall not discuss them right now.

After two introductory chapters Chris Lowney discusses six foundational commitments of Pope Francis as leader. They are (1) Know yourself deeply, (2) but live to serve others (3) Immerse yourself in the world (4) but withdraw from the world daily; (5) Live in the present and revere tradition (6) but create the future.[8]

If you examine these foundational principles carefully, you will see something paradoxical. "Each pair verges on being contradictory. I must be immersed in the world, yet withdraw from the world. I must stand for something, yet embrace change. I must invest in knowing myself only to transcend myself and serve others."[9]

1. Self-Knowledge and Self-Acceptance

The South African leader Nelson Mandela, who was kept in prison for more than two decades, once said: "My greatest enemy was not those who put me and kept me in prison. It was myself. I was afraid to be who I am."[10] It is difficult to believe this. He has always come across to us as a very self-confident leader.

A close acquaintance of Pope Francis once remarked: "That guy seems to be really comfortable in his own skin."[11] Pope Francis has a deep knowledge of himself and accepts himself fully. In an address from St Peter's Square he said. "Do not be afraid! We are frail and we know it, but he is stronger". Fr Hernan Parades, an Ecuadorean Jesuit, who was trained as a young Jesuit under Fr Bergoglio, has observed: "For him (Bergoglio) it was important that we love and accept ourselves the way we are". This was a powerful affirmation of Bergoglio's conviction that leaders must find peaceful self-acceptance, the conviction that "they have a worthy contribution to make, their flaws withstanding."[12] As Lowney points out:

> When you look into yourself, not everything you find will be pretty. Everyone is flawed: the demons of self-centredness, hunger for power, fear or lack of self-confidence are found in every leader. Leadership is, therefore, not only knowing yourself but also fighting your demons. If you have not courageously dealt with your weaknesses, and become

> the best version of yourself, how will you credibly challenge the rest of us to be better versions of ourselves.[13]

It is interesting to note that leadership literature over the past couple of decades has stressed the importance of these qualities: self-awareness, integrity, authenticity and character. "Self-awareness is the foundation of the others: I can be authentic, true to myself, only if I know myself, what I stand for, and what I ultimately think that humans are here for. And integrity is nothing more (or less) than understanding that I cannot honour such truths selectively: I must lead a "whole" life (the root meaning of integrity is "whole") not a split life."[14] Alejandro Gauffin, a Jesuit priest who studied under Fr Bergoglio, watched the Pope's first few days and then observed:

> Everything I see from the new pope now, everything I hear now...I saw then, and I heard then... It is like reliving our days together in the parish, when he taught me that gestures were worth much more than words.[15]

Commenting on Bergoglio's personal creed Lowney says: "Anyone familiar with Jesuit spirituality would immediately perceive how Bergoglio came by this worldview because the opening week of the Spiritual Exercises reinforces exactly the same dynamic."[16]

Introspection may appear to be a burden. Would not one be a better leader if one is not aware of one's insufficiencies? This is not true. Introspective impulse will liberate and empower a leader. Ultimately it will bring the blessing of self-acceptance or the courage to be oneself.

On the other hand, those leaders who have never practised introspection will go on making decisions and performing actions blissfully unaware of their weaknesses and the harm they cause to their families or organizations by their wrong decisions.

2. Commitment to Serve

As a Jesuit Fr Bergoglio sought to follow Jesus. This was inculcated in him by the Spiritual Exercises of St Ignatius. Now Jesus gave a powerful, even dramatic, demonstration of his determination to serve others. When Jesus and his disciples came together for the Last Supper, Jesus shocked everyone by what he did. As the evangelist John describes it: "Jesus poured water into a basin and began to wash the disciples' feet." The disciple Peter protested: 'you will never wash my fee't. He was quite embarrassed, and even outraged, that Jesus was doing something which at that time was performed only by slaves, in fact non-Jewish slaves, because such dirty work was thought to be beneath a Jewish slave's dignity. After Jesus had finished washing the feet of all his disciples present there he told them what he wanted them to do: "You call me Teacher and Lord – and you are right, for that is what I am. So if I, your Lord and Teacher, have washed your feet, you also ought to wash one another's feet" (Jn 13:13-14).

This shocking event is commemorated in Catholic churches all over world on Holy Thursday with selected men from the parish standing for the disciples and the parish priest for Jesus. The Pope does it at the Basilica of St John Lateran with select bishops or seminarians representing the apostles. By routinizing this gesture of Jesus the Church has made it a tame performance.

But Pope Francis recaptured some of the shock-value of feet-washing. On Holy Thursday in 2013 he did not go to St John Lateran. Instead he went to Casal del Marmo Juvenile detention centre and washed, wiped and kissed the feet of Juvenile delinquents. Some of them were Catholics, others non-Catholics. One was a Moslem woman. The Pope explained his action: "This is a symbol, it is a sign... Washing the feet means 'I am at your service....' As a priest and a bishop, I must be at your service."[17]

The Pope was here challenging not only Church leaders. Addressing "all those who have positions of responsibility in economic, political and social life, and all men and women of good will", Pope Francis said: "Let us never forget that all authentic power is service."[18] As Chris Lowney points out: "Good leaders see farther. They feel called to transcend themselves and serve a greater mission than self-interest alone."[19]

It is obvious that when unchecked ambition, careerism and self-interest run amuck it can negatively impact a leader's primary task of serving the people. St Ignatius was clearly aware of this danger. Hence, he devised means to form Jesuits in service mentality. One of the chief means was the meditation on the two standards that he developed in the Spiritual Exercises. In this meditation he asked the Jesuits to imagine the world as a battlefield where the followers of Jesus are pitted against those of Lucifer. I shall now quote Ignatius' description of the main elements of this meditation:

> Imagine you see the chief of all the enemy in the vast plain about Babylon, seated on a great throne of fire and smoke, his appearance inspiring horror and terror.
>
> Consider how he summons innumerable demons, and scatters them, some to one city and some to another, throughout the whole world, so that no province, no place, no state of life, no individual is overlooked.
>
> Consider the address he makes to them, how he goads them on to lay snares for men and bind them with chains. First they are to tempt them to covet riches (as Satan himself is accustomed to do in most cases) that they may the more easily attain the empty honours of this world, and then come to overweening pride.

> The first step, then, will be riches, the second honour, the third pride. From these three steps the evil one leads to all other vices.
>
> In a similar way, we are to picture to ourselves the sovereign and true Commander, Christ our Lord.
>
> Consider Christ our Lord, standing in a lowly place in a great plain about the region of Jerusalem, His appearance beautiful and attractive.
>
> Consider how the Lord of all the world chooses so may persons, apostles, disciples, etc., and sends them throughout the whole world to spread His sacred doctrine among all men, no matter what their state or condition.
>
> Consider the address which Christ our Lord makes to all His servants and friends whom He sends on this enterprise, recommending to them to seek to help all, first by attracting them to the highest spiritual poverty, and should it please the Divine Majesty, and should He deign to choose them for it, even to actual poverty. Secondly, they should lead them to a desire for insults and contempt, for from these springs humility.
>
> Hence, there will be three steps: the first, poverty as opposed to riches; the second, insults or contempt as opposed to the honour of this world; the third, humility as opposed to pride. From these three steps, let them lead men to all other virtues.[20]

In spite of his Jesuit training, Pope Francis knows that he is not totally immune to the demons of honour and pride. That is why he wrote to the Argentinian bishops asking for prayers that "I do not grow proud and always know how to listen to what God wants and not what I want"[21]

He also believes that his fellow priests and Church workers are not free from the allure of fame or riches. He sees the demons of clericalism and careerism at work in them. "These social climbers exist even in the Christian communities, no? Those people are looking out for themselves… They want glory for themselves."[22]

In a homily he preached on April 14, 2013, Pope Francis speaks of the idols in our life.

There are "many small or great idols that we have and in which we take refuge, on which we often seek to base our security. They are idols that we sometimes keep well hidden; they can be ambition, careerism, a taste for success, placing ourselves at the centre, the tendency to dominate others, the claim to be the sole masters of our lives, some sins to which we are bound, and many others… I would like a question to resound in the heart of each one of you, and I would like you to answer it honestly: Have I considered which idol lies hidden in my life…."[23]

Addressing the Pontifical Ecclesiastical Academy which trains priest-diplomats, Pope Francis warned them not to let their prestigious work go to their heads. 'Careerism is leprosy; Leprosy," he pointed out. He insisted that priests had to labour only for the "cause of the Gospel and the fulfilment of the mission", and "never for public recognition."[24]

3. Immerse yourself in the world's joys and sufferings

After he finished his term as the provincial of the Argentinian Jesuits, Fr Bergoglio was assigned to oversee the training of young Jesuits at Collegio Maximo San Jose'. The Collegio Maximo had a farm, the produce of which helped to support the financially straightened Jesuit community. All the members of the community worked on the farm. Herman Paredes, who was a Jesuit in training at that time, observes: "Bergoglio worked. I have in mind an image, one afternoon when I was coming back from the Parish where I was helping, seeing him there in his plastic boots, feeding the pigs."[25]

Though he was the rector of the Collegio Maximo Fr. Bergoglio did the laundry of the community. Fr. Thomas Bradley who was a Jesuit trainee remembers: "Already at 5.30 in the morning, Bergoglio would be placing clothes into those two industrial washing machines we had."[26] Apparently there were lots of clothes to wash, since there were more than a hundred of us living there.

Fr. Bergoglio "always insisted that the seminarians should go out at the weekends to offer (religious instruction) to the children. He said that someone who is able to make the catechism simple enough for a child to understand is a wise person."[27] And when the seminarians returned from the barrio, he "would to look to see if they had dusty feet. If they come back with clean feet he took it as a sign that they had done nothing."[28]

Around that time the bishop of Buenos Aires decided to start a new parish near the Jesuit seminary and asked Fr. Bergoglio to serve as its first pastor. The new parish priest drew up a crude map of the neighbourhood, divided it into zones and assigned seminarian volunteers to each zone. This is what he told the seminarians: "Get into the neighbourhood and walk it; don't comb the sheep, meet all of them, visit the poor and take care of their needs."[29]

Bergoglio instructed the seminarians: "You are going to learn from the people before you teach them anything". A few days after his papal election, he preached at the Chrism Mass on Holy Thursday in St. Laterano. Hundreds of priests gathered there. He exhorted them to be shepherds, "so deeply inserted in the midst of their sheep that they were living with the smell of the sheep."[30]

In an address to the Brazilian bishops Pope Francis raised a question:

> Unless we train ministers capable of warming people's hearts, of walking with them in the night, of dialoguing with their hopes and disappointments, of mending their brokenness, what hope can we have for our present and future journey?[31]

The Pope is convinced that "a Church that does not go out of itself, sooner or later sickens from the stale air of closed doors."[32] He also maintains that "we understand reality better not from the centre, but from the outskirts."[33] He firmly believes that "we cannot be starched Christians, too polite, who speak theology over tea. We have to become courageous Christians and seek out those who need help most."[34]

It is from the Spiritual Exercises that Pope Francis learnt not to withdraw from the world but plunge into it. For the world is a very good place, because it was created by God. And whatever God made is unfailingly good. It is also a world that has been redeemed by Jesus Christ. Besides, this world is the dwelling place of God. In the *Spiritual Exercises*' crowning meditation, St. Ignatius asks us to "consider how God dwells in creatures… in the plants, giving them life; in the animals, giving them sensation" According to Ignatius, God "dwells also in myself, giving me existence, life, sensation and intelligence; and even further, making me his temple…".[35]

This world-engaged attitude is the foundation of one of the great mantras of Ignatian Spirituality: "to find God in all things". It is interesting to note what one of his spiritual daughters, Soledad Albisu, said of Fr. Bergoglio:

> He took me outside where the community kept sheep and pigs. He told me that "this was a good place to pray and to remember that God is to be found in the lowliest things."[36]

4. Kneeling Alone: Withdraw to Find Perspective

On his first morning as Pope he knelt for fifteen minutes of solitary prayer at St Mary Major Basilica. Commenting on this Chris Lowney says: "The Pope was praying of course, but in the very act of praying he was recalling his sense of mission and the values he needs to keep and regaining perspective by acknowledging that the world is not ultimately under his control anyway."[37]

When he was in charge of Jesuit seminarians Fr. Bergoglio insisted on "a daily schedule of prayer, reading and reflection – and a commitment to sustaining and being punctual at it… in order to understand what is happening in one's life, and all the more so when one is going to be exposed to a very active life."[38]

As Lowney points out: "The pace, volume, complexity and volatility endemic to today's working life conspire to raise stress unimaginably, mire us in overwork, erode our decision – making skills, distract our focus and, as a result, threaten our very well-being."[39] In USA, the National Institute for Occupational Safety and Health believes that 40% of all workers feel overworked to the point of anxiety and depression.

Henry Mintzberg, a dean of modern leadership thinking, observes: "These days, what managers desperately need is to stop and think, to step back and reflect on their experiences."

Pope Francis has learnt from the Spiritual Exercises the practice of "examen of conscience". Jesuits practise it for fifteen minutes twice a day. During the examen "First You remind yourself why you are grateful as a human being; Second you lift your horizon for a moment by calling to mind your ultimate sense of purpose and values or some habitual failing you hope to address; And third, mentally review the past few hours to extract some insight that might help you in the next few hours. If you were irritable with colleagues or students or patients what might have been happening?" Jesuits also "reflect on how God was present to them in the encounters of the day thus far, make amends for their shortcomings and ask God's blessings on them during the next few hours."[40]

The practice of examen, which seems to be tailor-made to suit today's chaotic lifestyles, was in fact Ignatius of Loyola's ingenious solution to the dilemma presented by his highly active vision for Jesuit life:

> Ignatius envisioned his Jesuits fully immersed in the world as teachers, pastoral counsellors or missionaries in far – flung lands, getting their feet so dirty in the world's slums that they carried the smell of the sheep. That active lifestyle was incompatible with going to the chapel every few hours for communal prayer – the periodic chanting of the Divine Office, the hallmark of monastic-style religious orders. So the examen, undertaken individually, whenever and wherever circumstances permitted, would keep Jesuits recollected and God-focused, despite their activist lifestyle.[41]

Great leaders delegate, and delegate wisely. They know that they are not omni-competent. "Common sense tells us that no executive will understand every legal issue better than a competent legal counsel, or every manufacturing question better than an production pro."[42]

While delegating we may keep the following in mind: Give that person a realistic goal and the resources for it, but trust him/her to figure out how to accomplish it. He/she may be more creative than you.

Best results follow when the readiness to delegate is married to the ability to trust. Already in the 16th century St Ignatius was quite aware of this.

He sent Francis to Asia on a mission soon after the Society of Jesus founded in 1540. He relied completely on Francis' judgment to organize every aspect of Jesuit life and operations there.

Listen to Ignatius' words: "I leave everything to your judgement and I will consider best whatever you decide". Or again: "Whatever means you shall choose I fully approve… you are in closer touch with affairs where you are."[43]

This is a strong exercise of authority coupled with an equally bold delegation. Does the Pope show as much skill in delegating as his spiritual father Ignatius. As Lowney reports: "The cardinal-overseer of a key Vatican department, needing to fill the slot of a second-in-charge, recounted in an interview that the pope has asked him, "Who do you want as your secretary [i.e., your number two]? Give me three names." "So I gave him three names," the cardinal recounted. "But [the pope] said, 'Of the three, which is the one you want? I said this one, Carballo. [The pope] said, 'Good, fine.' And he gave us Jose Carballo [Jose Rodriguez Carballo, OFM]."[44]

The cardinal's next comment aptly summarizes our discussion of trust and delegation: "It's a wonderful, simple way of doing things: I trust you, I trust Carballo, so that's it.... He [the pope] doesn't complicate it."[45]

5. Live in the Present and Reverence Tradition

Life is short. Don't fritter it away on what is not important to you. Don't do what you might regret later. Conversely, seize each day's precious opportunity; one like it may or may not come your way. A coach tells the team: "Run like this is the last race you will run in your life."

Fr. Bergoglio first refused to hear the confession of a young man who looked quite disoriented, because he was in a hurry to catch a train. Then he changed his mind, heard the young man's confession and then prayed together with him.

There is a Jesuit mantra: *Age quod agis*. Do what you are doing. Dedicate yourself to what you are doing, and do it well. Fr. Bergoglio told the seminarians to strive for "excellence in their studies" and put in "demanding hours of daily study". He often said: 'We run the risk of scattering ourselves on too many directions."[46]

Jesuit Father Jean Pierre Caussade wrote a book: *Abandonment to Divine Providence* also known as the *Sacrament of the Present Moment*. In it he says:"There is not a moment in which God does not present himself under the cover of some pain to be endured, some consolation to be enjoyed or of some duty to be performed."[47] Fr. Bergoglio may have read this book.

Effective leaders commit themselves to the mysticism of the present moment. Yesterday's opportunity has passed, tomorrow's might not come, today's is waiting for me.

The present moment can never be divorced from the past. How I behave right now is an affirmation or rejection of what has been bequeathed to me by those who came before me: the values, culture, practices of my spiritual tradition, community or country.

Unfortunately, we sometimes imagine ourselves to be "Lords of history, nature and culture." It is not merely that we live in the present; it is as if what came before us never mattered. We free ourselves from the moral shackles of antiquated religious believes and outmoded customs of our grandparents. We insist on judging right and wrong by our own personal standards.

For Pope Francis "A Christian without memory is not a true Christian... he/she is a prisoner of circumstance, of the moment, a man or woman who has no history."

"When that happens, we find ourselves going from one experience to another without thinking and following the fashions of the time. We are reduced by temporariness."[48]

Pope Francis, who is relentlessly committed to seizing every present opportunity, understands that no leader effectively engages the present without some set of orienting values to distinguish one opportunity as more meaningful and worthwhile, moral or just than another.

In the Ordination Rite of a Deacon, he is asked to believe, teach and practise what he reads in the Gospel.

Inspiring are the leaders who believe, teach and practise – that is, leaders who stand for something. A Jesuit teacher of the seminary said of Fr. Bergoglio who was the Superior of the seminary: "I wasn't always in agreement with the way he was doing things, but I looked up to him. He had a vision, and he was committed to it."[49] In other words, he stood for something.

Pope Francis says: "Precisely if one is faithful one changes. One does not remain faithful, like the traditionalists or the fundamentalists, to the letter. Fidelity is always a change, a blossoming, a growth. The Lord brings about change in those who are faithful. That is Catholic Doctrine."[50]

He also said: "Memory of our roots, courage to face the unknown, capturing the reality of the moment."[51]

6. Create the Future: The Challenge of Leading through Change

In an address from St Peter's Square on 18 May 2013 Pope Francis asked: "What happens if we step outside of ourselves. The same as happens to anyone who comes out of the house and onto the street: an accident. But I tell you, I far prefer a Church that has had a few accidents than a Church that has fallen sick from being closed."[52]

Thomas Bradley was on summer duty in Collegio Maximo, a large seminary headed by Jorge Bergoglio. The Theology and Philosophy students had dispersed for summer. Bradley had studied agronomy. Yet he was assigned to do the Porter's duty, not to work in the farm. Why? Bradley gives two explanations: 1) Fr. Bergoglio "understood that we needed to develop an interior life in order to be effective in mission, in our work, and saw in the seminary's stillness an ideal school of the soul where an action-oriented young man could cultivate an increasingly rare skill: the ability to sit in solitude; 2) It is part of the spirituality of the Jesuits: one cannot always gravitate towards the work that one likes or what comes more easily; instead in order to live fully our Jesuit mission it is utterly essential that we learn to follow the path of detachment, of availability, of Ignatian indifference."[53]

Fr. Bergoglio told the young seminarians: "We have already made the hard decision (to become Jesuits). What for? We have to use that freedom."[54]

Bergoglio says: "Our orienting mission, goals, values and moral principles and the very sense of who we are as human beings often flow from traditioin. If we are free, those convictions pull us foreword and keep us properly oriented as a magnetic compass might."[55]

Fr. Bergoglio is ready to take risks. It is said that Bergoglio didn't have "shaky hands" in the face of tough choices. He made lots of them. He transferred to the care of trusted lay colleagues a Jesuit – run university in Buenos Aires and a school in Cordoba.

As Provincial Bergoglio sent some young Jesuits outside the country to shore up personnel-strapped Jesuit ministries in Ecuador – this at a time when Argentina was short of personnel. His explanation: "We Jesuits are not about guarding Jesuits (in our Province). We are about sending people in mission to wherever God's glory may be served, to wherever the need may be the greatest."[56]

It is not true that Fr. Bergoglio made every decision correctly. Leaders have to make judgements often amid uncertainties, under time pressure, and without a crystal ball for the future. The Pope confesses: "I have made mountains of mistakes."[57]

At the time of Cardinal Bergoglio's election as Pope, many Cardinals voiced discontent with the work of Vatican Headquarters. The German Cardinal Walter Kasper said: "The Curia must be revolutionized". What did Pope Francis do? He appointed a commission of eight Cardinals to advise him on Vatican reform. This was declared a revolution by a Vatican watcher Paulo Rodari.

It was certainly not a revolution for Pope Francis steeped in Ignatius' management vision. Jesuit rule book (the Constitutions) gave extraordinary decision – making authority to the Superior General and the Provincial Superiors.

Yet at the same time, the rule book stated "that leaders should have persons designated to give counsel, with whom they should consult on matters of importance which arise. When the system works well, the quality of the decision invariably improves. Leaders must articulate their rationale, say, for wanting to launch a new ministry or replace a key assistant. The consultors can probe for blind spots or derailing attachments that might be clouding the leader's judgement."[58]

By gathering smart advisors, the leader can mitigate his own weaknesses. In private comments that were later leaked to the press, the Pope revealed that such a motive had figured in his decision to convene the commission: "The reform of the Roman Curia is something that almost all cardinals asked for in the Congregations preceding the Conclave. I also asked for it. I cannot promote the reform myself, these are matters of administration…I am very disorganized, I have never been good at this. But the Cardinals of the Commission will move it forward…Pray for me…that I make the least possible mistakes."[59]

This is because the Pope has to make the final decision. Healthy leaders are secure enough to seek advice.

However, Pope Francis is not convinced that structural change alone will create a new Church. This is what he wrote in *Evangelii Gaudium*:

> There are ecclesial structures which can hamper efforts at evangelization, yet even good structures are only helpful when there is a life constantly driving, sustaining and assessing them. Without new life and an authentic evangelical spirit, without the Church's fidelity to her own calling, any new structure will soon prove ineffective.[60]

In his view a total commitment to mission and an earnest effort to fulfil it will transform the Church. In his own words, "I dream of a missionary option", that is, a missionary impulse capable of transforming everything, so that the Church's customs, ways of doing things, times and schedules, language and structures can be suitably channeled for the evangelization of today's world rather than for her self-preservation. The renewal of structures demanded by pastoral conversion can only be understood in this light: as part of an effort to make them more mission-oriented, to make ordinary pastoral activity on every level more inclusive and open, to inspire in pastoral workers a constant desire to go forth and in this way to elicit a positive response from all those whom Jesus summons to friendship with him. As John Paul II once said to the Bishops of Oceania: "All renewal in the Church must have mission as its goal if it is not to fall prey to a kind of ecclesial introversion."[61]

The Pope knows full well that an inward-looking Church will never change.

There are some clear indications that Pope Francis is going to change the Catholic Church. As Lowney points out:

> Well known for his dedication to Catholic tradition, Pope Francis started dispensing with tradition within minutes of his election, refusing the traditional red cape (mozzetta), placing his own phone calls, and hopping onto a bus instead of into the papal limo.

Further, He washes the feet of juvenile delinquents, kneels for fifteen minutes of solitary prayer on his first morning as pope, wears plain black shoes instead of red ones, wades into a crowd of refugees on the island of Lampedusa.

Besides, Pope Francis has chosen not to live in the papal palace. Instead he lives in a hostel..

Addressing young Catholics gathered in Rio de janeiro for World Youth Day Pope Francis stated:

> I want you to make yourselves heard in your dioceses, I want the noise to go out, I want the Church to go out onto the streets, I want us to resist everything to do with clericalism.... May the bishops and priests forgive me if some of you create a bit of confusion afterwards.[62]

Moreover, he challenged "lukewarm Christians" and "couch potato" Christians to engage much more energetically in spreading the Church's message, not to "take refuge....in a cozy life," but to get beyond our "comfort zones" and live with greater "apostolic fervour."[63]

- He challenged his Church to be more forthrightly "poor, and for the poor."[64]
- He warned Vatican diplomats –in-training that "careerism is leprosy."[65]
- He challenged a global culture in which "money… for the mighty of this earth, is more important than people."[66]
- He challenged his own fellow bishops to be "Men who love… poverty, simplicity and austerity of life."[67]

He asked Brazilian bishops bluntly, "Are we still a Church capable of warming hearts?[68] Cardinal Timothy Dolan of New York, reacting to the pope's challenges, told an interviewer, "I find myself examining my own conscience… on style, on simplicity, on lots of things."[69]

Notes

1. C. Lowney, *Pope Francis,: Why He Leads the Way He Leads,* Mumbai: St Pauls, 2014
2. *Ibid.* p. 23
3. *I bid.* p. 19
4. *Ibid.*
5. *Ibid.* p 24
6. *Ibid.* p 2
7. *Ibid.* p 29
8. *Ibid.* p. 21
9. *Ibid.* p. 22
10. *Ibid.* p. 43
11. *Ibid.* p. 47
12. *Ibid.* p. 48
13. *Ibid.Ibid.* p. 47
14. *Ibid.* p. 49
15. *Ibid.*
16. *Ibid.* p. 57
17. *Ibid.* p. 68
18. *Ibid.*
19. *Ibid.* p. 65
20. The Spiritual Exercises of St. Ignatius nos. 140-146
21. C. Lowney, *Pope Francis: Why He Leads the Way He Leads*, p. 79
22. *Ibid.* pp. 78-79
23. *Ibid.* p. 80
24. *Ibid.* p. 87
25. *Ibid.* p. 89
26. *Ibid.* p. 94
27. *Ibid.* p. 90
28. *Ibid.*
29. *Ibid.* pp. 97-98
30. *Ibi*d. p. 100
31. *Ibid.* p. 83
32. *Ibid.* p. 100
33. *Ibid.*
34. *Ibid.*
35. The Spiritual Exercise of St. Ignatius, no. 235

36. Chris Lourney *Pope Francis: Why He Leads the way He Leads*, p. 90
37. *Ibid.* p. 122
38. *Ibid.* p. 199
39. *Ibid.* pp. 113-114
40. *Ibid.* p. 123
41. *Ibid.* pp. 124-125
42. *Ibid.* p. 114
43. *Ibid.* p. 117
44. *Ibid.* pp. 117-118
45. *Ibid.* p. 118
46. *Ibid.* p. 140
47. *Ibid.* p. 145
48. *Ibid.* p. 148
49. *Ibid.* p. 149
50. *Ibid.* p. 158
51. *Ibid.*
52. *Ibid.* p. 161
53. *Ibid.* p. 163
54. *Ibid.* p. 165
55. *Ibid.*
56. *Ibid.* p. 168
57. *Ibid.* p. 170
58. *Ibid.* pp. 173-174
59. *Ibid.* p. 174
60. Pope Francis, *Evangelii Gaudium*, Rome, 2013, n. 26
61. *Ibid.*
62. *C. Lowney, Pope Francis* ... p. 15
63. *Ibid.* p. 17
64. *Ibid.*
65. *Ibid.*
66. *Ibid.*
67. *Ibid.*
68. *Ibid.*
68. *Ibid.*
69. *Ibid.*

3

BEFRIENDING THE OTHER

Vatican II and the New Orientations

In this chapter I shall contend that Vatican II has brought about radical changes in the Church's attitude to other Christian Churches, other religions and the modern world. These changes can be clearly seen if we keep in mind the totally different attitude which prevailed in the Church before the Council.

The situation of the Church during the last four hundred years (before Vatican II) was largely due to the impact of the Council of Trent. After pointing out that this Council succeeded in stemming the tide of the Reformation that threatened to destroy Catholicism and in starting a process of Church renewal, Giuseppe Alberigo observes:

But the price paid for this successful orientation cannot be overlooked; it can be summed up as a drastic isolation of Roman Christianity, now cut off and insulated from any interaction with the other Christian traditions of East and West, condemned to an attitude of defensiveness toward the modern world and, finally, surrounded by a *cordon sanitaire* to prevent contamination from alien cultures. Never in the history of Christianity had the *massa damnata* been made to include so much and so many; never had Christianity so extended and exacerbated its own estrangement from the fortunes of the human race.[1]

Trent has had an enormous impact on the Church for about four centuries. During this period the Church's isolation from the other Christian Churches grew. The struggle with the Protestant Reformation and the opposition to modern culture led to the development of "the 'closed' ecclesiology of the post-tridentine period in which the Church is a fortified castle, jealous of its purity and bristling with condemnations."[2] There was a strong resistance to all attempts break out of this fortress mentality and open up lines of communication with various cultures or to build bridges between the Church and the common human condition. The French Revolution and Vatican I only aggravated the situation. "Ecclesiocentrism thus reached levels that were new in relation to the entire Christian tradition."[3]

Looking back on the Council and carefully examining its documents one can clearly see that its basic thrust was the Church's recovery of the integral Christian tradition and the establishment of cordial relations to the other Christian Churches, the diverse religions and cultures of humanity and the modern world.

1. Befriending the Other Churches

1.1 From the beginning of Christianity divisions began to take place in the Church. These divisions led to the emergence of different Churches. By the middle of the 5th century all the churches other than the Graeco-Roman Church were shut out of the Catholic Church. In the 11th century the Greek Church got separated from the Roman Church. In the 16th century the Roman Church itself was split. As a result of the Reformation several churches came into existence – Lutheran Churches, Reformed Churches of Calvin, Zwingli and so on.

The reasons for division in the Church were many and varied. First of all, there were theological reasons. Sometimes, doctrinal differences paved the way for the emergence of new churches. Disciplinary matters too caused division. But there is reason to believe that social and cultural factors also caused division in the Church. This was quite evident in the separation between the Greek Church and the Roman Church. Diversity of culture may have played a role in Luther's revolt against Rome – the Germanic culture against the Latin culture. As Christopher Dawson has observed: "Most of the great schisms and heresies in the history of the Christian church have their roots in social and national antipathies, and if this had been clearly recognized by the theologians the history of Christianity would have been a very different one."[4] Joseph Neuner calls attention to another factor: "Luther's revolt is not primarily a theological challenge of traditional doctrines but a revolution against the domination of the Christian people through the clergy in a spirit totally alien to Jesus Christ."[5]

The way the Catholic Church reacted to the members of these churches was also alien to the spirit of Jesus Christ. They were condemned quite harshly.[6] In the Church there developed a feeling of animosity towards the members of these churches. They were anathema to the authorities of the Catholic Church.

1.2 All this changed with Vatican II**.** The Council sought to befriend non-Catholic Christians and their churches. It admitted that the division in the Church were caused both by the Catholics as well as non-Catholic Christians and hence "both sides were to blame."[7] In unmistakable terms Vatican II declared:

However one cannot impute the sin of separation to those who at present are born into these Communities and are instilled therein with Christ's faith. The Catholic Church accepts them with respect and affection as brothers and sisters. For men and women who believe in Christ and have been properly baptized are brought into a certain, though imperfect, communion with the Catholic Church. Undoubtedly the differences that exist in varying degrees between them and the Catholic Church – whether in doctrine and sometimes in discipline, or concerning the structure of the Church – do indeed create many and sometimes serious obstacles to full ecclesiastical communion. These the ecumenical movement is striving to overcome. Nevertheless, all those justified by faith through baptism are incorporated into Christ. They therefore have a right to be honoured by the title of Christian and are properly regarded as brothers and sisters in the Lord by the sons and daughters of the Catholic Church.[8]

In this text two statements are quite significant: (1) The Catholic Church accepts the members of these Churches with respect and affection; (2) They are properly regarded as brothers and sisters by the children of the Catholic Church.

This was the first step in the process of befriending non-Catholic Christians. The second step was to recognize the non-Catholic Christian communities as Churches. In an earlier draft of the Dogmatic Constitution on the Church there was a statement which totally identified the Church of Christ with the Roman Catholic Church." The Church of Christ is the Roman Catholic Church."[9] This was based on the teaching of Pope Pius XII that the Church of Christ, the Roman Catholic Church and the Mystical Body of Christ are one and the same thing.[10] The Council changed this statement to: "The Church of Christ subsists in the Roman Catholic."[11] It then observed that "many elements of sanctification and of truth can be found outside of her visible structure."[12] Whatever be the exact meaning of this changed formulation, it does imply that the Catholic Church does not exhaust the ecclesial possibilities of the Church of Christ. These ecclesial possibilities are realized in the other Churches. Hence, the Council calls them Christian Churches.[13]

The Catholic Church and these Christian Churches have many elements in common: Sacred Scripture, faith in the Triune God and Jesus Christ the Saviour. They celebrate baptism and some of the other sacraments. Many of them have the episcopate and venerate the Blessed Virgin Mary. These Churches have significance in the mystery of salvation. The Spirit of Christ uses them as means of salvation for their members.[14]

In its effort to befriend the other Churches, the Council took two more steps. While speaking about dialogue within and without the Church, Vatican II states: "Our hearts embrace also those brothers and communities not yet living with us in full communion."[15] The Council also expresses its desire to collaborate with the members of the other Churches:

Cooperation among all Christians vividly expresses that bond which already unites them, and it sets in clearer relief the features of Christ the Servant. Such cooperation, which has already begun in many countries, should be ever increasingly developed, particularly in regions where a social and technical evolution is taking place. It should contribute to a just appreciation of the dignity of the human person, the promotion of the blessings of peace, the application of gospel principles to social life, and the advancement of the arts and sciences in a Christian spirit.[16]

Such collaboration is to be extended to the fight against social evils like poverty and illiteracy. The Council goes on to add: "Through such cooperation, all believers in Christ are able to learn easily how they can understand each other better and esteem each other more, and how the road to the unity of Christians may be made smooth."[17]

2. Befriending the Other Religions

For centuries many Christians believed that Christianity was the only true religion since it alone was divinely instituted. Perhaps, the best known exponent of this view was Dr. Henrik Kraemer of Netherlands, who, in 1938, published a book titled: *The Christian Message in a Non-Christian World.*[18] "The main thesis of my book", he wrote in the Foreword, "is that the Christian Revelation is ... absolutely *sui generis.*[19] Following Barth and Kierkegaard, Kraemer maintains that there is an 'absolute qualitative difference' between the Gospel of Christ and all other religions. "When Christianity as a total religious system approaches the non-Christian religions as total religious systems, there is only difference and antithesis."[20] Hence, it is not possible to compare Christianity with any other religion. "There is no point of contact: ... there are no bridges from human religious consciousness to Christ."[21] Moreover, non-Christian religions are, according to this view, quite incapable of leading human beings to a true knowledge of God or of salvation.

And among Catholics a Church-centred ecclesiology held sway for a long period of time. According to this theology the Church was the only God-appointed means of salvation. There is no salvation outside the Church.[22] The Church possessed the fullness of truth and can teach it infallibly. She was the only authoritative interpreter of the natural law. By and large the Church's attitude to the other religions was quite negative. It was unthinkable that these religions might be ways of salvation for their followers. In 1867 Pius IX rejected as errors the following:

Everyone is free to embrace and profess the religion which by the light of reason he judges to be true. Men can find the way to eternal salvation and attain eternal salvation by the practice of any religion whatever.[23]

No wonder, then, that Catholic missionaries were not interested in dialogue and collaboration with the followers of other religions. Speaking of them E. C. Dewick has remarked:

> They went out with love for non-Christians in their hearts, but not with any thought of appreciating the non-Christian religions. Their purpose was simply to rescue souls from the clutches of heathenism in

this world and from the fires of hell in the next. They went to give, and not to receive; to save, not to cooperate.[24]

In all fairness it must be admitted that there were some Catholic thinkers like Cardinal Nicholas of Cusa who adopted a positive approach to the non-Christian religions. But they were not representative of the position generally held by Catholics.

It was in Vatican II that an Ecumenical Council for the first time dealt with the non-Christian religions. While discussing the schema on the Church the Council Fathers requested that non-Christians be treated not globally but according to the religious groups to which they belonged. Hence, *Lumen Gentium* deals with the Jews, the Muslims, those who believe in God and then the non-believers.[25] *Nostra Aetate* speaks of Hinduism, Buddhism, Islam and Judaism.[26] And Vatican II vindicates religious freedom not only for Christians but also for the followers of other religions.[27] Thus recognition is accorded to the world religions.

This is the first step in the Council's effort to befriend the other religions.

The second step is the expression of genuine appreciation of the positive values found in these religions – truth and goodness, grace and holiness.[28] Besides, Vatican II believes that God is the source of these values. According to the Dogmatic Constitution on the Church, "whatever goodness or truth is found among them is looked upon by the Church ... as given by Him who enlightens all men and women that they may finally have life."[29] Here, the text refers to John 1:9 which says that the Word was the true light which enlightens everyone. John is here speaking of the eternal Word and not the incarnate Word. The Decree on the Missionary Activity of the Church regards whatever truth and grace are to be found among the nations "as a secret presence of God."[30]

Hence for the Council these religions are not pure human creations. God is at work in their origin and growth. That is why Vatican II exhorts the children of the Church:

Prudently and lovingly, through dialogue and collaboration with the followers of other religions, and in witness of Christian faith and life, acknowledge, preserve, and promote the spiritual and moral goods found among these men and women, as well as the values in their society and culture.[31]

The Council looks upon dialogue as a means to arrive at truth through love and as a spiritual pursuit:

We also turn our thoughts to all who acknowledge God and who preserve in their traditions precious elements of religion and humanity. We want frank conversation to compel us all to receive the inspirations of the Spirit faithfully and to measure up to them energetically.

For our part, the desire for such dialogue which can lead to truth through love alone, excludes no one, though an appropriate measure of prudence must undoubtedly be exercised.[32]

The Council also encourages collaboration among the followers of different religions:

> Since God the Father is the origin and purpose of all men and women, we are all called to be brothers and sisters. Therefore, if we have been summoned to the same destiny, which is both human and divine, we can and we should work together without violence and deceit in order to build up the world in genuine peace.[33]

Thus, Vatican II looks upon the followers of other religions as partners in our common quest for justice and peace in the world.

3. Befriending the Modern World

Right from the beginning the Church's attitude to the world was ambiguous.[34] On the one hand it looked upon the world as an object of God's love, since God created it and continued to care for it. On the other hand it regarded the world as hostile to God, since it had closed itself against God in its sinful self-sufficiency. Both John and Paul, among the New Testament writers, gave expression to this ambiguity.[35] During the centuries of Roman persecution the Church adopted a very negative attitude to the world. It thought of itself as a community of believers surrounded by a wicked world.[36] Baptism was the moment of decision when a person renounced the spirit of the world and embraced the spirit of Christ.[37] The Didache has preserved a text which shows that the Eucharistic celebration concluded with the words: "Let grace come, let this world pass away.[38]

The Church of the Middle ages was somewhat ambivalent in its approach to the world. It fostered a spirituality based on a contempt of the world. As Alfons Auer has pointed out:

> The basic attitude of the Middle Ages was one-sidedly that of flight from the world. The monastic ascetical ideal prevailed also in the world; medieval Christianity was predominantly shaped by monks. Its ideal of life had a fascinating effect also upon laymen; one thought one could serve God best and most uncompromisingly when one bade farewell to the world.[39]

There was on the other hand an effort made to subjugate the world to the Church or even to absorb it. To quote Auer once again,

> In the greatness of the Middle Ages its very limitations become all the more apparent. No other age was able to achieve to the same degree a blending of the terrestrial and heavenly kingdom into a single universal order in which the temporal realms were directly ordered to the spiritual reality of the Church, and even – in order to maintain this order – directly or at least indirectly subjugated to ecclesiastical regulation. This unitary order necessarily resulted in a situation in

> which temporal matters were not adequately considered with respect to their inherent value nor sufficiently seen as fashioned according to their own laws. In the long run, the sacred order of the Middle Ages amounted to the same thing as Monophysitism.[40]

In a way the modern phenomenon of secularization is a reaction to this tendency on the part of the Church to absorb the world and not to respect it in its otherness. Gradually human beings, human society and its institutions, the arts and the sciences, work and professions began to assert their autonomy with respect to the Church and to affirm their intrinsic value. However, the Church reacted to this process quite negatively. As Avery Dulles observes,

The papal encyclicals from Gregory XVI (1831-46) to Pius XII (1939-59) continually deplore modern errors. *The Syllabus of Errors*, published by Pius IX in 1864, comes to a climax with Error No. 80: "The Roman pontiff can and should reconcile himself with, and adjust to progress, liberalism, and recent civilization." In 1907 the Church condemned Modernism, a movement that had begun as an effort by Catholics to bring the Church abreast of the times. Much later, just as World War II was breaking out, Pius XII issued his first encyclical, *Darkness over the Earth* (*Summi Pontificatus*, Oct. 20, 1939), reflecting remnants of this antimodernist mentality.[41]

Pope John XXIII had quite a different attitude. In his Apostolic Constitution convoking Vatican II he emphatically declared: "Distrustful souls see only darkness burdening the face of the earth. We, instead, like to reaffirm all our confidence in our Saviour, who has not left the world he redeemed."[42] And in his opening address to the first session he made it clear that he was not one of those who "in these modern times… can see nothing but prevarication and ruin."[43] Pope John's positive attitude to the modern world has had a great impact on *Gaudium et Spes*. That is probably why it has turned out to be one of the most inspiring documents of the Council.

Right at the beginning the Pastoral Constitution explains how it understands the modern world:

> Therefore, the Council focuses its attention on the world of men, the whole human family along with the sum of those realities in the midst of which that family lives. It gazes upon that world which is the theatre of man's history, and carries the marks of his energies, his tragedies, and his triumphs; that world which the Christian sees as created and sustained by its Maker's love, fallen indeed into the bondage of sin, yet emancipated now by Christ.[44]

There are three important elements in the Council's understanding of the modern world. This world is a world of human beings together with the subhuman creation in the midst of which they live. It is the scene of their history and bears the mark of their labour and their struggle, their successes and their failures. Though this world fell into sin it has been liberated by Christ. This is a very positive way of looking at the world. It is interesting to note that Vatican II regards the difficulties brought about by the rapid changes taking place in the world as a 'crisis of growth.'[45]

All this constitutes the first step in the Council's befriending of the modern world.

The second step is that Vatican II has adopted a positive attitude to the process of secularization. In unmistakable terms it declares:

If by the autonomy of earthly affairs we mean that created things and societies themselves enjoy their own laws and values which must be gradually deciphered, put to use, and regulated by men, then it is entirely right to demand that autonomy. Such is not merely required by modern man, but harmonizes also with the will of the Creator. For by the very circumstance of their having been created, all things are endowed with their own stability, truth, goodness, proper laws, and order. Man must respect these as he isolates them by the appropriate methods of the individual sciences or arts.[46]

Such a view leads to the recognition of the freedom and legitimacy of the arts and the sciences. As *Gaudium et Spes* puts it,

The Church is not against the use by human arts and sciences of their own principles and methods in their respective fields; therefore it acknowledges this lawful freedom and affirms the legitimate autonomy of culture and especially of the sciences.[47]

The third step that the Council has taken in befriending the modern world is this: It expresses its appreciation of the developments in the world:

The Council, therefore, looks with great respect upon all the true, good, and just elements found in the very wide variety of institutions which the human trace has established for itself and constantly continues to establish.[48]

Vatican II goes on to add:

> The Church further recognizes that worthy elements are found in today's social movements, especially an evolution toward unity, a process of wholesome socialization and of association in civic and economic realms. For the promotion of unity belongs to the innermost nature of the Church, since she is, "by her relationship with Christ, both a sacramental sign and an instrument of intimate union with God, and of the unity of all humankind."[49]

A fourth step is the manifestation of the Council's eagerness to dialogue with the modern world. It believes that "this Council can provide no more eloquent proof of its solidarity with the entire human family with which it is bound up, as well as its respect and love for that family, than by engaging with it in conversation about these various problems."[50]

In this context I would like to quote a pertinent observation made by Avery Dulles:

The Pastoral Constitution, in particular, sought to bring the Church into dialogue with the world on a basis of mutual respect and reciprocal give-and-take... The Council sees the Church as involved with the world in the tremendous social and cultural transformations of our times, and affirms the Church's solidarity with 'the joys and the hopes, the griefs and the anxieties of the men and women of this age'. Renouncing any attitude of haughty superiority, the Council expresses 'great respect' for "all the true, good and just elements found in the very wide variety of institutions which the human race has established for itself and constantly continues to establish". The Church here professes its readiness to put its talents and resources to work in order to contribute to secular goals such as peace, freedom, justice and human dignity.[51]

What is perhaps most significant in the Pastoral Constitution is that it conceives the role of the Church in the modern world as that of a servant. Inspired by no earthly ambition, the Church wishes only to carry forward the work of Christ who came not to be served but to serve.[52] Hence "Christians cannot yearn for anything more ardently than to serve the men and women of the modern world ever more generously and effectively."[53] The document spells out concretely the kind of service that the Church can render to human persons, human communities and human activity in the world.[54]

Yet another step in the Council's befriending of the modern world is this: it gratefully acknowledges the benefits the Church has received from the world. Vatican II has stated:

Thanks to the experience of past ages, the progress of the sciences, and the treasures hidden in the various forms of human culture, the nature of man himself is more clearly revealed and new roads to truth are opened. These benefits profit the Church, too.[55]

The Council goes on to add:

Since the Church has a visible and social structure as a sign of her unity in Christ, she can and ought to be enriched by the development of human social life. The reason is not that the constitution given her by Christ is defective, but so that she may understand it more penetratingly, express it better, and adjust it more successfully to our times.[56]

To conclude: The Second Vatican Council has taken several steps to befriend the non-Catholic Christians and their Churches, the followers of other religions and the modern world. It is upto the Catholic faithful now to imbibe the spirit of this great Council and establish cordial relations with non-Catholic Christians, the followers of other faiths and the modern world.

Notes

1. G. Alberigo "The Christian Situation after Vatican II" in G. Alberigo and others (eds.) *The Reception of Vatican II*, Washington, D.C.: The Catholic University of America Press, 1987, pp. 13-14.
2. *Ibid.*
3. *Ibid.* p. 15.
4. C. Dawson, *Dynamics of World History*, Wilmington: ISI books, 2002, p. 32.
5. J Neuner, "Exploring Global Dimensions of Jesuit Priestly Apostolate", *in Ignis Studies 2* (1983), p. 13.
6. Speaking of the members of the other churches the authorities of the Catholic Church use expressions like "perverse opinions and errors", "extraordinary boldness", "arrogant claim" etc. See Neuner –J. Dupuis, *The Christian Faith*, Bangalore, TPI, 2008, n. 816.
7. Vatican II, Decree on Ecumenism, n. 3.
8. *Ibid.*
9. Vatican II, Dogmatic Constitution on the Church, n. 8.
10. See Neuner-Dupuis, *The Christian Faith*, nos. 847, 858.
11. Dogmatic Constitution on the Church, n. 8.
12. *Ibid.*
13. *Ibid.*, n. 15; Decree on Ecumenism, n. 3.
14. Decree on Ecumenism, n. 3.
15. Vatican II, Pastoral Constitution on the Church in the Modern World, n. 92.
16. Decree on Ecumenism, n. 12.
17. *Ibid.*
18. H. Kraemer, *The Christian Message in a Non-Christian World*, London: 1938.
19. *Ibid.*, p. IX.
20. *Ibid.*, pp. 130, 300; see also pp. 115-120.
21. *Ibid.*, pp. 131-132.
22. See Neuner-Dupuis, *The Christian Faith*, n. 810.
23. *Ibid.* n. 810.
24. E. C. Dewick, *The Christian Attitude to Other Religions*, London: Cambridge, 1953, p. 116.
25. See Dogmatic Constitution on the Church, n. 16.
26. See Vatican II, Declaration on the Church's Relationship to Non-Christian Religions.
27. Vatican II, Declaration on Religious Freedom n. 4.
28. See Dogmatic Constitution, n. 16; Decree on Priestly Formation, n. 16; Declaration on the Church's Relationship to Non-Christian Religions, n. 2.
29. Dogmatic Constitution on the Church, n. 16.
30. Decree on the Missionary Activity, n. 9.
31. Declaration on the Church's Relationship to Non-Christian Religions, n 2.
32. Pastoral Constitution on the Church in the Modern World, n. 92.
33. *Ibid.*
34. See J. Neuner, "The Role and Responsibility of the Laity in the struggle for a New Society" in D. S. Amalorpavadass, (ed.), *The Indian Church in the Struggle for a New Society*, Bangalore: NBCSLC, 1981, pp. 44-49.
35. See J. L. Mckenzie, *Dictionary of the Bible*, pp. 942-944.
36. See J. Neuner, "The Role and Responsibility of the Laity", p. 448.
37. See E. Schillebeeckx, *Ministry: A Case for Change*, London: SCM Press, 1981, p. 56.
38. Didache, 10, 6.

39. A. Auer, "The Changing Character of the Christian Understanding of the World", in *The Christian and the World" Readings in Theology*, compiled by Canisianum, Innsbruck, 1965, p. 6.
40. *Ibid.* pp. 8-9.
41. A. Dulles, *Models of the Church*, Garden City: 1974, p. 31.
42. Pope John XVIII, Apostolic Constitution "Humanae Salutis" dated Decembere 25, 1961, convoking the Council. See W. R. Abbot, *Documents of Vatican II*, New York: America Press, 1966, p. 704.
43. Ibid., p. 712.
44. Pastoral Constitution on the Church in the Modern World, n. 2.
45. *Ibid.*, n. 4.
46. *Ibid.*, n. 36.
47. *Ibid.*, n. 59.
48. *Ibid.*, n. 42.
49. *Ibid.*
50. *Ibid.*, n. 3.
51. A Dulles, "The Church is Communication" in *Catholic Mind*, 69 (1971), p. 11.
52. Pastoral Constitution, n. 3.
53. *Ibid.*, n. 93.
54. *Ibid.* nos. 40-43.
55. *Ibid.*, n. 44.
56. *Ibid.*

4

FREEDOM AND JOY

Recently I had a chat with some college students who had just finished their retreat. During the conversation the students said that to watch a movie is a serious sin. So, too, drinking some vine or paying a visit to a Hindu temple. I was quite puzzled at what they said. So I asked them how they knew all this. They answered: "Our retreat master told us".

I wonder if unenlightened retreat preachers tend to curtail the freedom of young people and deprive them of joy in their Christian life. I am quite convinced that freedom and joy are essential characteristics of our Christian existence. I shall now explain the basis of my conviction. Let me begin with the freedom.

1. Jesus and freedom. After a careful investigation of the Kingdom of God which was central to the life and ministry of Jesus the great Scripture scholar George Soares-Prabhu has come to the conclusion that Jesus was the supreme example of the freedom of the Kingdom of God. He has stated:

> Jesus moves through the pages of the Gospel as the supremely free man. He is driven by no demons of greed or ambition – for the Son of Man "has nowhere to lay his head" (Lk 9:58) and has come "not to be served but to serve" (Mk 10:45). He is daunted neither by the pressures of heteronomous law (Jn 8:1-10) nor by the violence of established authority (Lk 13:31-33). With supreme freedom he challenges the most sacred institutions of his people when his concern for his fellowmen impels him to do so. He breaks the Sabbath (Mk 7:1-15), touches lepers (Mk 1:42), dines with the socially outcast and with sinners (Mk 2:15-17).[1]

Jesus believed that it was his mission to liberate people. He said that the Spirit of the Lord "has sent me to proclaim release to captives and recovery of sight to the blind, to let the oppressed go free" (Lk 4:18). Jesus frees human beings from sin and guilt (Mk 2:1-12). He frees us from the routine of ritualism (Mt 6:7) and from the oppressive burden of the law (Mt 11:28-3 and 23:4). He liberates us from the terrible isolation to which we can be condemned by social ostracism (Lk 19:1-10), ritual uncleanness (Mk 1:40-45) or mental ill-health (Mk 5:1-21). He calls his followers to freedom from possessions (Mk1:16-18; 10:1) from unhealthy family ties (Lk 9:61). He invites them to put all their trust in God so that they need no other security in life (Mt 6:25-34).

As a result of his personal encounter with Jesus Paul exclaims: "For freedom Christ has set us free. Stand firm, therefore, and do not submit again to a yoke of slavery (Gal 5:1).

Vatican II has dealt with freedom in the Pastoral Constitution on the Church in the Modern World. It declares that "authentic freedom is an exceptional sign of the image of God in a human being". Then it adds: "For God has willed that man be left in the hand of his own counsel" so that he can seek his Creator spontaneously, and come freely to utter and blissful perfection through loyalty to him."[2]

In 2013 Pope Francis, in his Apostolic Exhortation, The Joy of the Gospel, stated:

Saint Thomas Aquinas pointed out that the precepts which Christ and the apostles gave to the people of God "are very few". Citing Saint Augustine, he noted that the precepts subsequently enjoined by the Church should be insisted upon with moderation "so as not to burden the lives of the faithful: and make our religion a form of servitude, whereas "God's mercy has willed that we should be free."[3] This warning, issued many centuries ago, is most timely today.

Our great concern should be not to make the Christian religion a religion of unfreedom.

Here, I would like to recall the powerful words of St Paul: "For you were called to freedom, brothers and sisters" (Gal 5:12). The implication of these words is this: Freedom is God's gift to us. Every gift of God involves a task on our part. Hence it is our lifelong task to become increasingly more free. But as a famous hymn has it: "It is a long road to freedom."

It is, therefore, the duty of the Church to impart an education for freedom to all its members.

2. Joy

When Jesus was born in Bethlehem an angel of the Lord told the shepherds: "I am bringing you good news of great joy for all the people" (Lk 2: 10). In the gospel of Mark Jesus begins his public ministry by proclaiming the good news that the Kingdom of God has come (Mk 1:14-15). Now joy is one of the fruits of the Kingdom (see Rom 14:17). Towards the end of his ministry Jesus declared: "I have said these things to you so that my joy may be in you and that your joy may be complete" (Jn 15:11). After a careful examination of the life and ministry of Jesus, Albert Nolan came to the conclusion:

Joy was in fact the most characteristic result of all Jesus' activity amongst the poor and the oppressed. The meals he had with them were festive celebrations, parties. Jesus obviously had a way of ensuring that people enjoyed themselves at the gatherings. The Pharisees were scandalized by this. Rejoicing and celebrating with sinners was incomprehensibly scandalous (Lk 15:1). They could only assume that he had become a pleasure –seeker, 'a drunkard and a glutton' (Lk 7:34)."[4]

Jesus tried to explain this joy and this celebration to the Pharisees by telling them three parables: The parables of the lost sheep, the lost coin and the lost son (Lk 15). It is highly significant that each of these parables ends with joy and celebration. When the shepherd finds his lost sheep, he calls together his friends and neighbours and celebrates with them. And Jesus adds: "Just so, I tell you, there will be more joy in heaven over one sinner who repents than over ninety-nine righteous persons who need no repentance" (Lk 15:6-7). Something similar happens when the woman finds her silver coin which was lost. (15:9-10). The last parable is extremely significant. After listerning to the parable one wonders: Who is the lost son? The younger son who went away from the Father and lived riotously with his women? Or the elder son, who, like a true Pharisee, kept the law most faithfully? The younger son was able to receive God's forgiving love, rejoice in it and celebrate it. But the elder son was not able to do so. So, he is really the lost son! To quote Nolan once again: "There can be no doubt that Jesus was a remarkably cheerful person and that his joy like his faith and hope was infectious... The poor and the oppressed and anyone else who was not too hung up on 'respectability' found the company of Jesus a liberating experience of sheer joy."[5]

Pope Francis points out that the whole Bible speaks of joy. We shall now look at some of the texts from the New Testament. The angel tells Mary: "Rejoice". When Mary visited Elizabeth "the child in her womb leaped for joy (Lk 1:41). In the Magnificat, Mary declares: "My spirit rejoices in God my Saviour" (Lk 1:47). At the beginning of Jesus' ministry John cries out: "For this reason my joy has been fulfilled" (Jn 3:29) Jesus himself "rejoiced in the Spirit" (Lk 10:21). He promises his disciples: "You will be sorrowful but your sorrow will turn into joy" (Jn 16:20). Then he adds: "But I will see you again, and your hearts will rejoice, and no one will take your joy from you" (Jn 16:22). The disciples "rejoiced" at the sight of the risen Lord. In the Acts of the Apostles we read that the first Christians "ate their food with glad and generous hearts" (Acts 2:46). Because of the preaching of Philip and the miracles he worked "there was great joy in that city" (Acts 8:8). The newly baptized eunuch "went on his way rejoicing" (8:39), while Paul's jailer "and his entire household rejoiced that he had become a believer in God" (Acts 16:34).

This experience of joy of the first Christians should inspire all of us to find great joy in our Christian life.

Unfortunately, "there are Christians whose lives seem like lent without Easter." Some of them walk through life as though they are taking part in a perennial funeral procession. But the Church shows that joy is the abiding quality of Christian. In the middle of Lent, which is popularly thought of as a time of repentance and penance, the Church breaks into joy. The liturgy of the fourth Sunday of Lent (which used to be called *Laetare* Sunday) begins with the verse: "Rejoce with Jerusalem, and be glad for her, all you who love her; rejoice with her in joy, all you who mourn over her – that you may drink deeply with delight from her glorious bosom" (Is 66:10). This reveals the Church's awareness that joy, and not sadness, is the abiding quality of Christian life.

Pope Francis invites Christians everywhere "to a renewed encounter with Jesus Christ". For "with Christ joy is constantly born a new."[6]

Christian mission too demands happy evangelizers. Pope Francis is quite sure that "an evangelizer must never look like someone who has just come back from a funeral.[7] In this context the Pope quotes the words of Paul VI.

Let us recover that enthusiasm, that "delightful and comforting joy of evangelizing, even when it is in tears that we must sow....And may the world of our time, which is searching, sometimes with anguish, sometimes with hope, be enabled to receive the good news not from evangelizers who are dejected, discouraged, impatient or anxious, but from ministers of the Gospel whose lives glow with fervour, who have first received the joy of Christ."[8]

Notes

1. G. Soares-Prabhu "The Kingdom of God: Jesus' Vision of a New Society, in F. D' Sa (ed.) *Collected Writings of George M. Soares – Prabhu*, Vol. 4, Pune: JDV, 2001, p. 239.
2. Vatican II, Pastoral Constitution on the Church in the Modern World, Rome, 1965, n. 17.
3. Pope Francis, *Evangelii Gandium*, Rome, 2013, n. 43.
4. A Nolan, *Jesus Before Christianity*, London: Darton, Longman and Todd, 1977, pp. 41-42.
5. *Ibid.* n. 42.
6. Pope Francis, *Evangelii Gaudium,* n. 1.
7. *Ibid.* n. 10.
8. *Ibid.*

5

FREEDOM FROM OWNERSHIP

Recently I read a thought-provoking article in the Times of India titled: "Freedom from Ownership: A very different kind of existence."[1] The article was written by Santosh Desai. I shall now briefly summarise the article and then reflect on it. There are some important points that Desai makes in the article.

1. There was a time when ownership was highly appreciated. As the author expresses it:

   To own things was the source of the greatest joy as well as being a mark of achievement. Gharbasana, the idea of setting up home, was the painstaking accumulation of objects that gave stability and meaning to life. One's place in the world got cemented by virtue of ownership. Owning things did nothing more than establish exclusivity of the right to use the thing in question, but its social meaning was so much more. One grew as one owned; the thing that one acquired became part of an expanded definition of the self.[2]

   The prevalent idea was this: The more you have the more your are.

2. People are becoming increasingly disillusioned with the idea of ownership. Ownership has begun to appear as a burden.

   As Desai puts it: To own is also to simultaneously be owned. Objects occupy space; they weigh heavy and need minding. The act of driving through insane traffic, with gritted teeth and knitted brow, is part of the cost that ownership imposes on us.

   And then in the case of cars, there is the question of parking. There is something cruelly metaphorical about not finding a way to extricate oneself from one's owned object. The car becomes an annoying appendage, a clingy pest that cannot be shaken off. The burden of ownership is never as heavy and as frustratingly cumbersome as it is when one is looking for a parking spot on a busy day in the city.[3]

3. People are starting to prefer usership to ownership. "The new app based providers of transportation like Uber and Ola have revolutionized the lives of many". There are quite few people today who are thinking about doing without a car. And that is not because they can't afford it. We need to reflect on this phenomenon. Here, Desai makes a perceptive comment:[4]

   > At a conceptual level, what does it mean for the idea of ownership? It is interesting that the idea of getting what we want when we want it seems to be becoming a higher form of possession. It raises an improbable question-what is it that we really want when we seek to own something? For ownership is at its heart really about control – that an object is ours to do as we please with it, at a time and place of our choosing. The new models of usership seem to deliver to this brief. The object in question now corresponds exactly to our desire. We get a taxi when we want it to take us where we need to go. It is in this preciseness of alignment between impulse and its satisfaction that a new definition of consumption is taking birth.

4. Gradually ownership is losing its attraction. As Desai observes: "The Joy of being able to own things begins to lose meaning in a surplus society, where the ability to afford things has no specialness attached to it. Consumption becomes mechanical, and the excitement of owning things needs to be drummed up."[5]

   All the same we find it difficult to throw away things.
5. The decrease in the desire to possess things expands the self. According to Desai: "The declining desire for ownership potentially produces a surplus of the self. Without the baggage of attachment to things, there is more of oneself to go around. The self becomes infinitely divisible; imagine an infinite wardrobe, where one could wear the clothes of one's choice whenever one felt likes it."[6]
6. Today there is a growing awareness that we don't have to own everything we need. In the words of Desai: "There is a new grammar of desire that is beginning to take shape, and the implications that will unfold as a result are likely to transform how we think about and lead our lives. To be free of belongings is to imagine a very different kind of world."[7]
7. Now we need to reflect on the implications of all this for our Christian existence. There are three important points we need to keep in mind.

   7.1 Jesus and Ownership. In unmistakable terms Jesus declares that he does not own anything: "Foxes have holes, and birds of the air have nests; but the Son of Man has nowhere to lay his head", (Lk 9:58).

   Speaking of Jesus' public ministry George Soares – Prabhu states: "Jesus 'declasses' himself and adopts of the life of an itinerant peacher without a home or means of subsistence."[8] And "he dies utterly poor and totally outcast on the cross."[9]

Jesus' person and lifestyle are a challenge to all his followers.

7.2 Discipleship and Ownership

In the Gospel of Luke Jesus declares: "Blessed are you who are poor..." (6:20). Then he adds: "Woe to you who are rich". Jesus has a great appreciation for the poor but not for the rich.

In this Gospel there is the story of the rich ruler who asks Jesus: "What must I do to inherit eternal life?" (18:18) And Jesus tells him to keep the commandments of God. The ruler says: "I have kept all these since my youth". (18:21). Then Jesus tells him: "There is still one thing lacking. Sell all that you own and distribute the money to the poor, and you will have treasure in heaven; then come, follow me" (18:22).

In order to be a follower of Jesus, a person has to divest himself/herself of all his possessions. Ownership of great possessions and discipleship of Jesus Christ cannot coexist. Jesus makes ths abundantly clear: "So therefore, none of you can become my disciple if you do not give up all your possessions" (Lk 14:33). This is confirmed by the account of Jesus' call of his first disciples. This is how Mark narrates it:

As Jesus passed along the sea of Galilee, he saw Simon and his brother Andrew casting a net into the sea-for they were fishermen. And Jesus said to them, "Follow me and I will make you fish for people." And immediately they left their nets and followed him. As he went a little farther, he saw James son of Zebedee and his brother John, who were in their boat mending the nets. Immediately he called them; and they left their father Zeb'e.dee in the boat with the hired men, and followed him. (Mk 1:16-20)

Note that the response of those called to be disciples is whole-hearted and total. They left everything and followed Jesus. In fact Peter would declare a little later: "Look, we have left everything and followed you" (Mk 10:28).

Is it realistic to expect that all Christians who are supposed to be disciples of Jesus will really renounce all their possessions? In answer to this question I would like to say three things:

1) To be a disciple of Jesus one does not need to live in misery. We have a right to make use of the good things of life to live, to grow and to fulfil our mission in life.
2) Christians have to make serious efforts in order not to be slaves of riches. Of rich Christians Jesus declares: "It is easier for a camel to go through the eye of a needle than for someone who is rich to enter the kingdom of God" (Matt 19:24).

Camel was the largest animal that Jesus has seen (He never saw an elephant) and the eye of a needle was the smallest hole that Jesus knew. Hence, message is quite clear: It is practically impossible for a rich person to enter the Kingdom of God.

3) An unmistakable sign that a Christian is not a slave of his possessions is this: The readiness to share his riches with the poor and the needy. The Christian tradition has always maintained that the wealth of the world is for all humankind. As Vatican II has stated: "God intended the earth and all that it contains for the use of every human being and people"[10]

7.3 The Religious Life and Ownership

Through the vow of poverty the religious renounce ownership and embrace a life of poverty. Most of the founders and foundresses of religious congregations practised real poverty and asked their followers to do the same.

But the tragedy of the religious life is this: Within fifty years of their foundation most religious congregations became rich. As a justification for this state of affairs there developed an interpretation of the vow of poverty: Every member of the congregation observes the vow of poverty strictly, but the congregation can amass any amount of wealth. The spiritual writers and the theologians of the Church have not seriously reflected on the community dimension of the vow of poverty. Besides, rich communities/congregations make it increasingly difficult for individual members to practise poverty. As Karl Rahner once observed: "No one can be poor if he/she belongs to a rich community."[11]

Before her death Mother Teresa (now Saint Teresa) of Kolkata was asked: What would happen to your congregation after your death. She answered: "If my Sisters are quite strict in the observance of the vow of poverty, the congregation will flourish. Otherwise it will perish".

Many years ago I used to work with some Sisters in the outskirts of Vienna, Austria. These Sisters called themselves: Sisters of the poor Child Jesus. But the people referred to them as the rich Sisters of the poor Child Jesus. The fact of the matter is that money-mindedness has crept into religious congregations quite noticeably. As a result, the spirit of selfless service that characterized their apostolate at the beginning has almost totally disappeared. The craze for ownership is quite widespread. In this connection I would like to make two observations:

1) In the context of globalization the question of ownership has become quite critical. Global capital has placed us before a choice: God or Mammon. Mammon is wealth when we part our trust in it. But Jesus has warned us: "You cannot serve God and Mammon" (Matt 6:24).
2 The Letter to Timothy has powerfully affirmed: "For the love of money is the root of all kinds of evil" (1 Tim 6:10).

Notes

1. S. Desai, "Freedom from Ownership: A Very Different Kind of Existence" in *The Times of India*, Pune, February 6, 2017, p. 6.
2. Ibid.
3. Ibid.
4. *Ibid.*
5. *Ibid.*
6. *Ibid.*
7. *Ibid.*
8. G Soares-Prabhu, "The Spirituality of Jesus" in S. Kuthirakattil (ed.), *Collected Writings of G. M. Soares Prabhu*, Vol. 3, p. 93.
9. *Ibid.,* p. 94.
10. Vatican II, Pastoral Constitution on the Church in the Modern World, Rome, 1965, n. 69.
11. K. Rahner, "Theology of Poverty" in *Theological Investigations*, Vol. VIII, p. 172.

6

CHRISTIAN MISSION IN INDIA TODAY

During the Easter season (April 2017), I was reading and reflecting on the Gospel accounts of the resurrection of Jesus Christ. Three things struck me: 1. There was no eyewitness to resurrection itself; 2. During his Easter appearances the risen Lord was quite gracious to the disciples who had deserted him during his passion; 3. There is a mission command in all the four gospels. It is as though Jesus Christ were telling the disciples: Now that I am not visibly present in the world, you should help me to fulfil my God – given mission. And I shall be with you always to help and guide you. In this paper I wish to examine these mission texts in some detail. I would like to do it in the context of India.

I. India Today

Instead of a comprehensive analysis of the Indian situation I shall merely highlight three important dimensions of the Indian reality which I think will enable us to understand our Christian mission quite adequately:

1) Massive Poverty.
   In spite of the marvellous growth the Indian economy has achieved during the last 25 years, there is widespread poverty in our country. Two things are significant about poverty in India. a. Though it is difficult to get adequate statistics, most people believe some 250 to 300 million people live below the poverty line. In history no country has housed as many poor people as India does today. b. Poverty in India is human-made. Now our country has the resources to remove poverty from the face of India. And yet it will not be done because the ruling elite has no political will to do so.
2) Communal disharmony.
   For centuries the followers of different religions of India lived together in peace and harmony. But what we witness today are religions in conflict.

For a variety of reasons communal hatred and violence are growing in our country. There is some evidence that after Bharatiya Janata Party came to power at the Centre in May 2014 there is a significant increase in communal clashes in India.

3) Growing violence.
The land of the peace-loving Mahatma is fast becoming a slaughterhouse in which innocent people are mercilessly butchered everyday. There is a lot of violence in Kashmir and in the Northeast. The criminalization of politics and the political involvement of criminals have caused the growth of violence. Nowadays cow-protection groups are torturing and murdering people who are falsely suspected of selling and eating beef.

II. Mission Commands

1. In the Gospel of Mark

In chapter 16 the Risen Lord issues the command: "Go into all the world and proclaim the good news to the whole creation" (Mk 16:15). What does the "good news" mean? To understand it we have to go to chapter one where it is said: "Jesus came to Galilee, proclaiming the good news of God and saying, The time is fulfilled, and the kingdom of God has come near" (Mk 1:14-15). The good news is that the kingdom has come, that God is savingly present among us. The kingdom of God is God's definitive offer of salvation to humankind.

After a careful investigation, the well-known Scripture scholar George Soares-Prabhu has come to the conclusion: "The kingdom of God is Jesus' vision of a new society."[1] Taking into account all that the Gospels say about the kingdom of God we can affirm: The Kingdom of God is a new human society which is consciously rooted in God, which is characterized by equality, freedom, love, justice, peace and joy, and which lives in harmony and communion with the cosmos. This society has three relationships: It is consciously rooted in God. All created reality is rooted in God, but the members of this society deliberately, consciously, acknowledge their total dependence on God. It has a healthy relationship to the cosmos, it lives in harmony and communion with the whole cosmos. In this society the members relate to one another in freedom and equality, love and justice, peace and joy.

We help to build the kingdom of God when we teach and encourage people to have deep faith in God and when promote kingdom values like freedom and equality, love and justice. In this connection I wish to quote two significant statements of Pope John Paul II:

1) Working for God's kingdom means acknowledging and promoting God's activity which is present in human history and transforms it.[2]
2) Through the Gospel message, the Church offers a force for liberation which promotes development precisely because it leads to conversion

> of heart and of ways of thinking, fosters the recognition of each person's dignity, encourages solidarity, commitment and service of one's neighbour, and gives everyone a place in God's plan, which is the building of His Kingdom of peace and justice, beginning already in this life.[3]

2. In the Gospel of Matthew

In the last chapter the Risen Lord commands the apostles: "Go therefore and make disciples of all nations, baptizing them in the name of the Father and of the Son and of the Holy Spirit and teaching them to obey everything that I have commanded you" (Mt 28: 19-20). What does it mean when Jesus asks us "to make disciples of all nations". It means much more than just baptizing people and entering their names in the Parish register. It demands that we take steps to give a proper Christian initation to the people who wish to join the Church and impart to them an adequate Christian education.

Who is a disciple of Jesus? Different Gospels give different answers to this question. The Gospel of Mattew makes it clear that in order to be a disciple of Jesus two things are required: 1. The renunciation of all wealth. To a scribe who wished to follow him Jesus says: "Foxes have holes, and birds of the air have nests; but the Son of Man has nowhere to lay his heads" (Matt 8: 20-21)). And Jesus tells the rich young man who was eager to gain eternal life: "Go, sell your possessions, and give the money to the poor and you will have treasure in heaven; then come, follow me". Therefore if one really wants to be a true disciple of Jesus one has to renounce all his possessions and then follow Jesus; 2. The practice of unconditional love. In the Sermon on the Mount Jesus commands: "Love your enemies and pray for those who persecute you... For if you love those who love you, what reward do you have? Do not even tax collectors do the same? And if you greet only your brothers and sisters, what more are you doing than others"? Be perfect as your heavenly Father is perfect", (Matt 5: 44-48). "Here perfection does not mean flawlessness but wholehearted and undivided commitment to God's project for humanity. The disciples are called to live by Jesus' teaching, revealing God's unconditional love and graciousness."[4]

It is the Church's mission to nurture such disciples of the Lord.

3. Mission in the Gospel of Luke

The Risen Lord said to the disciples: "Repentance and forgiveness of sins is to be proclaimed in his name to all nations, beginning from Jerusalem. You are witnesses of these things. And see, I am sending upon you what my Father promised; so stay here in the city until you have been clothed with power from on high," (Lk 24 : 47-49).

In the Gospel 'to repent' is expressed by the Greek word *metanoein* which means "to change one's mind". But underlying this word is the Hebrew idea of conversion *'Shub'* which involves the turning of the whole person to God (see Is 31: 6; Jer 3:12-14; Hos 41:1). If you take the Greek and Hebrew understandings of repentance together, repentance involves a threefold change: 1. A cognitive change = adopting a new vision of life and reality; 2. An attitudinal change = acquiring a new set of values; 3. A behavioural change = assuming a new a way of acting, behaving.

It is part of the revelation given in Jesus Christ that our God is not an angry, avenging deity but a God of mercy and compassion who forgives sinners. Hence, Jesus gives us the mission to proclaim in his name forgiveness of sins.

But forgiveness has a larger meaning than the forgiveness of human sin. John Paul II has pointed out that forgiveness is absolutely necessary for world peace:

> But no process of peace can ever begin unless an attitude of sincere forgiveness takes root in human hearts. When such forgiveness is lacking, wounds continue to fester, fuelling in the younger generation endless resentment, producing a desire for revenge and causing fresh destruction. Offering and accepting forgiveness is the essential condition for making the journey towards authentic and lasting peace.[5]

There is a third element in the mission command of the Risen Lord. He tells the disciples that they will receive the Holy Spirit, the promised of the Father, and be empowered for mission. This takes us to chapter 4 of the Gospel where Jesus reads a passage from Isaias and applies it to himself:

> The Spirit of the Lord is upon me because he has anointed me to bring good news to the poor. He has sent me to proclaim release to the captives and recovery of sight to the blind, to let the oppressed go free, to proclaim the year of the Lord's favour." And he rolled up the scroll, gave it back to the attendant, and sat down. The eyes of all in the synagogue were fixed on him. Then he began to say to them, "Today this scripture has been fulfilled in your hearing." (Lk 4:18-21).

Jesus believes it to be his mission to set people free – to liberate people from all that prevents their growth and happiness: from sin and corruption, from poverty and ignorance, from hunger, disease and death. Now the disciples are anointed with the Holy Spirit to carry on Jesus' mission of liberation.

Unfortunately we human beings cannot make anyone free. All that we can and should do is to remove obstacles to the full exercise of freedom and create conditions in which people will feel free.

4. Mission in the Gospel of John

On the day of Resurrection Jesus told the apostles: "As the Father has sent me, so I send you"(Jn 20:21). So we have the same mission as Jesus. The term mission comes from the Latin *missio* which is the noun form of the verb *'mittere'* which means to send. So we have the same sending, mission, as Jesus.

How does Jesus understand his mission. In chapter 10 of the Gospel Jesus declares: "I came that they may have life, and have it abundantly". (Jn 10:10). Jesus believed it to be his mission to bring an abundance of life to people-life in all its dimensions. And we have received the same mission from the Lord.

Every day each one of us must ask himself/herself: Am I a life-giving person? One of the ways in which we can promote life is by teaching and encouraging people to make choices that are life-enhancing. Listen to what Deuteronomy has to say:

> See, I have set before you today life and prosperity, death and adversity. If you obey the commandments of the LORD your God that I am commanding you today, by loving the LORD your God, walking in his ways, and observing his commandments, decrees, and ordinances, then you shall live and become numerous, and the LORD your God will bless you in the land that you are entering to possess (Deut 30: 15-16).

I have often wondered if the washing of the feet in John 13 has implications for our Christian mission. After washing the feet of the disciples, Jesus tells them:

> So if I, your Lord and Teacher, have washed your feet, you also ought to wash one another's feet. For I have set you an example, that you also should do as I have done to you. Very truly, I tell you, servants are not greater than their master, nor are messengers greater than the one who sent them. If you know these things, you are blessed if you do them, (Jn 13: 14-17).

Will it be alright if I interpret these words of Jesus thus: It is part of our Christian mission to render humble, lowly service to our brothers and sisters?

5. Mission in Paul

The Risen Lord entrusted his mission to Apostle Paul who did not belong to the original twelve apostles whom Jesus chose. After he was knocked down while he was on his way to Damascus Paul was told by the Risen Lord: "But get up and enter the city, you will be told what you are to do" (Acts 9:6). It is through Ananias that Paul will come to know his mission. Jesus tells Ananias: "Go, for he (Paul) is an instrument whom I have chosen to bring my name before Gentiles and kings and before the people of Israel" (Acts 9:15).

Paul's mission work has two elements: 1. Promoting faith (Rom 1:5). Paul was quite convinced that human beings are justified by faith and not by the works of the law (see Rom 3: 27-30). Hence, he worked energetically to persuade the Gentiles to have faith in the God of Jesus Christ, the Saviour. 2. Fostering reconciliation. Paul was quite conscious that he had received the message and ministry of reconciliation from the Lord (see 2 Cor 5: 18-20). Reconciliation has two dimensions-reconciliation of people with God and reconciliation of people among themselves (see Eph 2: 13-16).

Now reconciliation has relevance beyond the Church, for all humankind. The Church should take up the ministry of reconciliation in a big way. Pope John Paul II has asked the bishops and priests of the Church to be instruments of peace and reconciliation "not only in the ecclesial community, but also in civil society where nationalistic and ethnic conflicts are raging."[6] He also appealed to all "the members of the Church to be devoted in an active and practical way to the work of the reconciliation."[7] In the conflictual situation of India today, the appeal of the pope takes on a note of great urgency.

Now to sum up what has been said above. According to the testimony of all the four evangelists the risen Lord gave a mission mandate to his apostles/ disciples.

In the Gospel of Mark the risen Lord asks the apostles to go into all the world and proclaim the good news. The good news is that the kingdom of God has come near, that in Christ Jesus God is making a definitive offer of salvation to all humankind. Faith is the response of people to the good news. In the Gospel of Matthew the Lord commissioned the apostles to make disciples of all nations. Now making disciple of people involves something more than baptizing them and entering their names in the parish register. It calls for giving them a proper Christian initiation and imparting to them a truly Christian education. In the Gospel of Luke the risen Lord commanded the disciples to proclaim in his name repentance and forgiveness of sins to all nations. Forgiveness is a necessary condition for lasting peace. In the Gospel of John the risen Lord gives the same mission as he has received from Father. It is a mission to be life-giving and growth-promoting people. From the risen Lord Paul received the mission to foster faith among the Gentiles. He is also given the ministry of reconciliation – reconciliation between people and God as well as reconciliation among people.

The mission to bring about reconciliation has a relevance beyond the boundaries of the Church in the civil society. In the conflictual situation of India/ the world today the Church is called to be an agent of reconciliation and peace.

Notes

1. George M. Soares–Prabhu, S.J "The Kingdom of God: Jesus' Vision of a New Society" in Francis X D' SA (ed:), *Collected Writings of George M. Soares – Prabhu, S.J. Vol 4*, Pune: JDV, 2000, p. 223.
2. John Paul II, *Redemptionis Missio*, n. 15.
3. *Ibid.*, n. 59.
4. R. A. Chennattu, "Disciple" in E. D' Lima, S.J (ed.), in*A Concise Encyclopedia of Christanity in India*, Pune: JDV, 2014, p. 362.
5. John Paul II, "Message for the World Day of Peace 1997" in *The Pope Speaks*, 42 (1997) p. 169.
6. John Paul II, "Message for the World Day of Peace 1997" in *The Pope Speaks*, 42 (1997) p. 175.
7. *Ibid.*, p. 173.

7

FORMATION OF PRIESTS IN INDIA TODAY

Some Observations

I have been on the staff of a seminary for about 45 years. Hence, most of what I am going to say here is based on my personal experience. Besides, I have done some reading and made a lot of reflection on formation. All that I wish to say can be summed up in five statements. They may be called theses.

1. One cannot be a good priest, an effective pastor, if one is not a good human being.

One can possibly be a good doctor or a good lawyer even if one is not a good human being. But no one can be a good priest if he is not a good man. For the life and ministry of a priest is concerned with the quality of human/Christian life.

Besides, the priests' ministry will not be effective, fruitful, if he does not command the respect of the people. And the people will not respect a priest who is not honest, not a man of integrity and who does not deal with people with justice and fairness. Further, Vatican II encourages the priest to strive to acquire good human qualities. After briefly describing the goals of priestly ministry, the Council goes on to state:

In the achievement of these goals, priests will find great help in the possession of those virtues which are deservedly esteemed in human affairs, such as goodness of heart, sincerity, strength and constancy of character, zealous pursuit of justice, civility, and those other traits which the Apostle Paul commends, saying: "Whatever things are true, whatever honourable, whatever just, whatever holy, whatever lovable, whatever of good repute, if there be any virtue, if anything worthy of praise, think upon these things" (Phil 4:8).[1]

2. A large number Catholics in India do not believe that the majority of priests are honest men, men of integrity.

This statement is based on the sociological studies of priests in India by Paul Parathazham.[2] According to him, priests "were generally rated low also on basic human qualities like integrity (honest, straight forward and trustworthy), justice and fairness (no favouritism and discrimination), and commitment to truth."[3] In concrete, only 56% of the lay people think that the majority of priests are honest men, men of integrity while only 35% of the nuns and 49% of the clergy think so. 50% of the laity believe that the majority of priests are just and fair in their dealings with people, while only 37% of the religious sisters and 49 percent of the clergy believe so.[4]

To be honest, I find these findings quite disturbing.

3. There is a crisis of values in the seminaries today.

Paul Parathazham made an all India survey of formators of the priests and the religious. Summing up his findings Parathazham states: "It should be noted that, according to the formators, the majority (of the formees) lack not merely the specific religious orientations like prayerfulness and spiritual depth, but also basic human qualities like integrity, openness and transparency, and commitment to justice."[5] Concretely, 50 percent of the respondents think that only some or a few of the formees are persons of character and integrity. What is even worse is this: 55 percent of them believe that only some or a few are committed to justice.

From my long years in the seminary I can say two things: 1. Some seminarians lack intellectual honesty. They tend to copy in the examinations, because of which invigilation has become necessary in written examinations. 2. They need to strengthen their moral values. Some of them are not always transparent with money. They misappropriate the books of the library. They use vulgar language and indulge in loud talk and shouting. They lack, at times, sensitiveness to the feelings of others.

4. The cultural situation of our country and the family background of the seminarians will help us to understand the crisis of values in the seminary.

In spite of the enormous economic and scientific progress India has made in recent decades, our country is, I believe, in a state of moral disintegration. The idealism of the leaders of our freedom struggle and the moral integrity of the Founding Fathers of the Indian Republic have all disappeared.

> There is now naked power struggle in the political arena. There is corruption in high places. Bureaucrats, army officers, judges, ministers and chief ministers have all been found guilty of corruption. Some of our business leaders engage in amoral practices. Think of all the scams we have witnessed in recent years. And then there is the scandalous life of some of our religious leaders.
>
> All this has a great impact on the young seminarians who are born and brought up in this atmosphere. Perhaps even more decisive is the influence

of the family. For the family, as Joe Mannath points out, "is the best and most influential formation house. Most of our formation is over by the time we reach the seminary". It has been found that by the age of six a person's basic personality is set and his life orientations are fixed.

Hence, it is important to ask: What are the values a seminarian has internalized during his early childhood? There are no scientific studies which will help us to answer this question.

There are two factors which we need to keep in mind.

1) It is very likely that the cultural situation of our country has an impact on the families of our seminarians. They will find it quite difficult to escape the corrupting influence of society. There is one experience of mine which may throw light on the values that prevail in our families. I know of a few cases where Catholic parents sent their sons/daughters to a seminary or a novitiate of the religious merely to learn good English. After about two years they are called back and sent for secular studies. I still find it very difficult to understand how Catholic parents can do this in good conscience. But they do.
2) The other thing is this: The majority of seminarians today come from lower middle class and poor families. It is true that they are really representative of the Church since the vast majority of Catholics in India are poor. All the same, there is a problem. As Paul Parathazham has observed: "This development, however, poses new challenges to formation. It increases the likelihood of mixed motivation in the candidates, since the priesthood may appeal to them also as a channel of social and economic mobility."[6]

Thus, the cultural situation in the country as well as in the family tends to have a corrupting influence on the young seminarian.

5. We urgently need to take steps to form priests who are good human beings and effective pastors.

I shall suggest three steps that can be taken. 1) Encourage the seminarian to make a passionate commitment to his personal growth. Help him to become deeply aware of the negative impact of the unhealthy culture prevailing in the family and the country. And make him take responsibility for his personal growth.

2) Enable the seminarian to make creative use of living groups. The Charter of Priestly Formation in India has recommended that large seminary communities be divided into small groups. Quite a few seminaries have made small living groups the units of formation. From my personal experience, I can say that small living groups in which the seminarians feel accepted and loved and are allowed to be truly themselves are a great help to emotional growth. Besides, personal counselling, group dynamics and group-therapy have been found helpful in promoting personal growth.

Further, seminarians need to develop the ability to be totally transparent in the living group. Psychologists speak of self-knowledge through self-disclosure. Seminarians also need to master the art of non-aggressive confrontation.

3) Encourage the seminarians to cultivate a spirituality that humanizes, that makes them good human beings.

My impression is that there is a lot of piety among the seminarians but not enough spirituality. Piety consists in the performance of external devotional practices and is measured by one's fidelity to these practices. Whether or not the faithful performance of these exercises of piety improves the quality of one's Christian life is a question that is seldom asked. One is at times surprised that priests, sisters and lay people who are obviously pious are manifestly unfair in their dealings with other people. Some of them show so little of the compassion of Christ and are quite unwilling to forgive others.

> But spirituality is a way of life. It is our total inward quest for growth, meaning and authenticity. And it is manifested in the quality of one's life. In the last analysis, to be spiritual is to be touched and transformed by the Spirit of God. In a person who has been touched and transformed by God's Spirit the fruits of the Spirit will be seen: "love, joy, peace, patience, kindness, generosity, faithfulness, gentleness and self-control" (Gal 5: 22-23). Besides, "where the Spirit of Lord is, there is freedom" (2 Cor 3:17).
>
> Vatican II says: "Whoever follows after Christ becomes more of a human being."[7] To follow Christ is to become increasingly more human. Speaking of the humanity of Christ, the Council states: "He worked with human hands, He thought with a human mind, acted by human choice and loved with a human heart. Born of the Virgin Mary, He has truly been made one of us, like us in things, except sin."[8] That is why the followers of Christ have to be human too. "Indeed, nothing human fails to raise an echo in their hearts."[9]
>
> To strive to be more fully human and to cultivate truly human qualities enables them, to be good human beings and effective pastors. As Pope John Paul II has pointed out:
>
> Further, priests should therefore cultivate a series of human qualities, not only out of proper and due growth and realization of self, but also with a view to the ministry. These qualities are needed for them to be balanced people, strong and free, capable of bearing the weight of pastoral responsibilities. They need to be educated to love the truth, to be loyal, to respect every person, to have a sense of justice, to be true to their word, to be genuinely compassionate, to be men of integrity and especially, to be balanced in judgement and behaviour.[10]

Notes

1. Vatican II, Decree on the Ministry and Life of Priests, Rome, 1965, n. 3.
2. See P. Parathazham, *Christianity in India: Sociological Investigations*, Bangalore: Dharmaram Publications, 2013, pp. 103-127.
3. *Ibid.* p. 120.
4. *Ibid.* pp. 118-121.
5. *Ibid.* p. 233.
6. P. Parathazham "Issues in Priestly Formation": A Question of Credibility" in *Vidyajyoti* 58/1994, p. 713.
7. Vatican II, Pastoral Constitution on the Church in the Modern World, Rome, 1965, n. 41.
8. *Ibid.* n. 22.
9. *Ibid.* n. 1.
10. Pope John Paul II, *Pastores Dabo Vobis, Rome,* 1992, n. 43.

8

THE EXPERIENCE OF GOD

The experience of God is at the origin of the Church. Just as Israel originated from the experience of the liberating God in the exodus event, so too the Christian Church sprang up from the experience of the saving God in the life, death and resurrection of Jesus Christ. In his Apostolic Exhortation, *Ecclesia in Asia*, Pope John Paul II asks the Church to be ever "more deeply rooted in the experience of God which flows from a living faith."[1]

It is in this context that I wish to discuss the question of the experience of God.

1. In Christian tradition as well as in Hindu tradition God is believed to be incomprehensible to our finite minds. He is also ineffable. Thus, God is beyond our thoughts and words.

   Therefore, when we speak of the experience of God we are not making statements about God, but about us, about the change, the transformation, that takes place in us as a result of encountering God. The Sanskrit term *anubhava* probably means the same thing.

2. Whenever and wherever there is an upsurge of life, growth, freedom, love, justice, unity, peace and joy, there has been an experience of God.

   In his letter to the Galatians Paul compares and contrasts flesh and Spirit. Flesh refers to a human being in a state of sin, the unredeemed person, who is "subject to earthly tendencies" whereas the Spirit points to the human being who is open to God, the redeemed person, "who is under the influence of God's Spirit."[2] Hence he/she has been touched and transformed by God's Spirit. In such a person you can find the fruits of the Spirit – "love, joy, peace, patience, kindliness, generosity, faithfulness, gentleness and self-control"(Gal. 5: 22). Freedom too is a fruit of the Spirit for "where the Spirit of the Lord is, there is freedom" (2 Cor 3: 17). I am inclined to believe that it is the experience of God, of God's Spirit, that transforms a person and produces in him/her the fruits of the Spirit.

3. As Charles Davis points out, in the religious traditions of humankind there are at least four ways in which people have encountered the Divine.[3] First of all, there is the experience of God in nature, of God as the power behind natural phenomena. The experience of God in nature often leads to faith in natural gods. This is found in Hinduism from the days of the Vedas. Vayu, Agni and Surya are some of the gods of the Hindus. Such an experience of God is also found in the Christian tradition (see Rom 1:20). Secondly, there is the experience of God in the depths of one's being. This leads to the cultivation of interiority. God – ward journey often takes an inward direction. Such an experience is described in the Upanishads. Something similar is found among the Christian mystics. St. Augustine maintains that God is more intimate to me than I am to myself. Thirdly, there is the experience of God mediated through the rites and doctrines of a religion. This is probably the most valued form of God-experience in popular Catholicism where there is a great insistence on the frequent reception of the sacraments as well as orthodoxy in the profession of faith. The Hindus, too, have samskaras which mediate God-experience. Fourthly, there is the experience of God in inter-human relationships, in socio-political involvements. This form of God-experience is typical of the biblical tradition. The foundational God-experience of Israel was the Exodus - the experience of God in the liberation of slaves. Israel also experienced God as the One who was active in the decisive moments of its history. And the early Christians experienced God in the life, death and resurrection of Jesus who was done to death as a political criminal. For us Christians, the human person is the privileged locus of God-experience. We encounter God first of all in Jesus of Nazareth, and then in every man, woman and child. As Charles Davis concludes: "The Christian religion has always been thoroughly political, with social and political action the major vehicle of the distinctly Christian religious experience. Briefly, Christians find God in their neighbour rather than in their inner consciousness or in the cosmos."[4]

4. The Second Vatican Council has a similar approach to the experience of God. In the Pastoral Constitution on the Church in the Modern World, the Council states: "The people of God believes that it is led by the Spirit of the Lord who fills the earth. Motivated by this faith, it labours to decipher the authentic signs of God's presence and purpose in the happenings, needs and desires in which this people has a part along with other men and women of our age."[5] What Vatican II says is this: God is present and expresses his intentions in the events and experiences of people today. Hence, it is possible for them to encounter God in and through these events and experiences.

The Council goes to add: "For their part, however, believers of whatever religion have always heard His revealing voice in the discourse of creatures."[6] In this connection it is good to recall the meaningful observation of Gabriel Moran: "People who demand that there be a higher norm of truth than human experience are asking for an idol. Man has no recourse in his life except to turn to what is finite. He can submit, as he is always tempted to submit, to a text or a ruler or an institution built by his own hands. There is no lack of things available and waiting for divinization. His only other alternative is to follow his own human experience and to pursue it wherever it takes him. If there be a God, must not his voice be heard within the experience of a man who listens with all other men for the voice of the divine".

5. One can experience God present and active in the depths of one's being. This is the way I experience it. When someone shouts at me I am tempted to shout back at him/her, but a gentle voice within me tells me not to. When someone does me wrong, my natural tendency is to hit back. Again I hear a soft voice within me urging me not to. Yet again, when I am hurt by someone's words or actions and am eager to do something hurtful to him/her there is an inner voice asking me to be patient and forgive. To me these are some of the ways in which I experience God.

6. How is one to initiate people into an experience of God?

   It must be quite clearly understood that experiencing God is not something that a person does, but something that happens to him/her. Hence all that a person can do is to take steps to dispose himself/herself for an experience of God.

   The first step is to cultivate deep inner silence and true solitude. In today's world not many people are fond of silence and solitude. Ours is a noisy world and lots of people want other people to entertain them. On the wall of a monastery is written: Solitude is the home of saints and silence is their language. This is a welcome reminder to all of us that silence and solitude are absolutely necessary for anyone who wishes to experience God.

   The next step is to develop deep awareness. Such as awareness is essential for anyone who wishes to find how God is present and active in the depths of one's being.

   This leads to the next step: discernment. In his book, *The Spiritual Exercises*, St. Ignatius Loyola makes these observations:

   It is characteristic of God and His Angels, when they act upon the soul, to give true happiness and spiritual joy, and to banish all the sadness and disturbances which are caused by the enemy.

God alone can give consolation to the soul without any previous cause. It belongs solely to the Creator to come into a soul, to leave it, to act upon it, to draw it wholly to the love of His Divine Majesty. I said without previous cause, that is, without any preceding perception or knowledge of any subject by which a soul might be led to such a consolation through its own acts of intellect and will.[7]

Finally one needs to observe the social reality. God who is present and active in the hearts of human beings is present and active in human society. Hence, to read the signs of the times means to decipher the signs, the manifestations, of God's presence and activity in the world of our times.

By way of conclusion I would like to say this: The only unmistable sign of the genuineness of one's God-experience is a transformed life. If anyone really experiences God, that experience will lead to a significant improvement in the quality of his/her life. There will be an increase in faith, hope and love as well as a life lived according to the values of the Gospel.

Notes

1. John Paul II, *Ecclesia in Asia*, New Delhi, 1999, n. 23.
2. See J. A. Fitzmyer, "Commentary on the Letter to the Galatians" in R.E. Brown and others (eds.), *The New Jerome Biblical Commentary*, Prentice Hall, 1990, p. 789.
3. C. Davis, "From Inwardness to Social Action: A Shift in the Focus of Religious Experience", in *New Blackfriars* 67 (1986). pp. 114–115.
4. *Ibid.* n. 122.
5. Vatican II, Pastoral Constitution on the Church in the Modern World, Rome, 1965, n. 11.
6. *Ibid.* n. 36.
7. L. J. Puhl (ed) *The Spiritual Exercises of St. Ignatius*, Chicago; Loyola University Press, 1952, nos. 329-330.

9

SENSITIVITY TO THE OTHER

The Example of the Good Samaritan Man

The parable or example of the good Samaritan man is valid even today. A careful examination of the text shows that there are two distinct episodes in **Luke 10:25-37**: (1) A pronouncement about the double commandment of love; (2) the story of the Good Samaritan. These episodes seem to have existed separately in the Jesus' tradition which Luke received. By introducing the lawyer's question: Who is my neighbour?, Luke makes an attempt to connect the two episodes. But the attempt is not very successful since the parable of the Good Samaritan does not really answer the lawyer's question.

The Story of the Samaritan Man

Though the story of the Good Samaritan is often called a parable, it is better understood as an example (an "exemplum" in Rhetoric). It provides a practical model for a Christian conduct which responds to the radical demands of the Gospel. It also includes the approval or the disapproval of certain modes of behaviour.

Crucial to the understanding of the story are certain significant details:

1. The privileged status of the priest and the Levite in Palestinian Jewish society. Their Levitical heritage associated them intimately with the Temple cult and the heart of Jewish life as worship of Yahweh.
2. Defilement thought to be derived from contact with a dead or an apparently dead body. The priest and the Levite passed by on the other side in order to avoid contamination by contact with a dead body.
3. The attitude of the Palestinian Jews towards the Samaritans is summed up so well by John 4/9: Jews use nothing in common with the Samaritan

(non *coutuntur*). Their history made them schismatics in the eyes of the Jews, and relations with them were far from cordial.

These details underlie the story's basic contrast: the compassion and kindness shown by a schismatic Samaritan to an unfortunate human victim stands out vividly against the heartless, law-inspired insensitivity of two official representatives of the Jewish religion. Thus, the point of the story is summed up in the lawyer's reaction, that a 'neighbour' is anyone in need with whom one comes in contact and to whom one can show compassion and kindness, even beyond the bounds of one' own ethnic or religious group.

Sensitivity to the Other

The story of the Good Samaritan raises some questions for us. I shall discuss just three of them:

1. What is the place of law in our life? Or what influence does it exert on our behaviour?

The priest and the Levite in the story were insensitive men because of their fidelity to the laws regarding defilement. But the regulations on defilement from contact with a dead body were also to be found in the Samaritan Pentateuch, but they did not prevent the Samaritan from being sensitive and helpful to a person in need. His compassion and kindness enabled him to transcend such restrictions. His love and concern goes beyond all rules and regulations.

We are disciples and ministers of Jesus who declared that Sabbath is for humankind. Sabbath was indeed the highest religious law of the Jews, but Jesus subordinated it to the welfare of the human person. What would be for us a healthy attitude to law which does not prevent us from being sensitive and helpful to people in need? This question needs an honest answer.

2. Is insensitivity to people in need a vocational hazard of priestly/religious life? Because of the kind of training we have received, because of the style of life we have adopted, do we inevitably tend to be blind and deaf to the cries of people in agony? As priests we are called to be mediators between God and people. We are meant to be signs, sacraments, of God's presence and activity in the world. Yet we seem to be quite different from the God of the Exodus who says:

I have seen the affliction of my people who are in Egypt, and have heard their cry because of their taskmasters; I know their sufferings, and I have come down to deliver them out of the hand of the Egyptians and to bring them to a good and broad land, a land flowing with milk and honey... (Exodus 3:7-8).

3. Do we tend to be communal in our social concern? Is our approach to the problems and needs of people too much Church-centred?

In the Gospel passage when the lawyer speaks of the commandment to love your neighbour as yourself he is quoting Leviticus 19:18. In the context neighbour means a fellow Israelite. Let me quote the two verses immediately before 19:18:

> You shall not go around as a slanderer among your people, and you shall not profit by the blood of your neighbour: I am the Lord. You shall not hate in your heart anyone of your kin; you shall reprove your neighbour, or you will incur guilt yourself (Lev 19:16-17).

But the Samaritan who is held up as a model for us does not primarily think of himself as a Samaritan but as a human being. Hence for him the important thing was not that a Jew was in need of help but that a human being was. In this context let me quote the perceptive comment of Pope Benedict XVII (now *Emeritus*):

The parable of the Good Samaritan (cf. Lk 10:25-37) offers two particularly important clarifications. Until that time, the concept of "neighbour" was understood as referring essentially to one's countrymen and to foreigners who had settled in the land of Israel; in other words, to the closely-knit community of a single country or people. This limit is now abolished. Anyone who needs me, and whom I can help, is my neighbour. The concept of "neighbour" is now universalized, yet it remains concrete. Despite being extended to all humankind, it is not reduced to a generic, abstract and undemanding expression of love, but calls for my own practical commitment here and now.[1]

Concluding Remarks

We live in a country where the pride of one ethnic or religious group forces another group to develop an equally false and divisive pride of it own; when the selfishness of one group forces another group to develop a selfishness of its own. It is here that we are called upon to practise the universalism of Christian love. We believe that the object of God's love is the whole world, that Jesus Christ died not just for Christians but for all human beings. This demands that we be sensitive to the problems and needs of everyone, that we be at the service of all. As Vatican II declares: "Christians cannot yearn for anything more ardently than to serve the men and women of the modern world ever more generously and effectively."[2] (*GS* 93).

It is here that we see the significance of the double commandment of love which in Luke serves as a preface to the story of the Good Samaritan. It is only when we really love people, only when we are genuinely interested in and concerned about their problems and needs that we can truly be sensitive to them. Thus we can be sensitive to the Other in their Otherness.

Notes

1. Emeritus Pope Benedict XVI, *Deus Charitas Est*, Rome, 2005, n.15
2. Vatican II, Pastoral Constitution, on the Church in the Modern world, Rome, 1965, n. 93

10

THOUGHTS FOR TEACHERS

These thoughts are primarily meant for professional teachers. But probably they are relevant to all adults who in one way or another are teachers in life if not in the classroom. Then why should we exclude children who are in some way teachers?

As C.P. Varkey has pointed out, "the role of the teacher in education will remain paramount. He or she alone can create the congenial climate for learning."[1] Child psychologist Dr. Haim Gonott, who was once a teacher, agrees with C.P. Varkey. In his book, *Teacher and Child*, he declares: "I have come to a frightening conclusion. I am the decisive element in the classroom. It is my personal approach that creates the climate. It is my daily mood that makes the weather. As a teacher I possess tremendous power to make a child's life miserable or joyous. I can be a tool of torture or an instrument of inspiration. I can humiliate or humour, hurt or heal. In all situations it is my response that decides whether a crisis will be escalated or de-escalated, and a child humanized or de-humanized."[2]

Recently I came across a letter an anonymous student wrote to an unknown teacher. Most of my reflections here are related to what the student wrote in that letter.

1. The letter begins with a plea: "Try to be a human being, not just a teaching machine. Do not teach only the subject, but rather teach us students. Let me feel that you are interested in me as a human being, not just a number in your note-book".

   There are three important points in this plea. 1) A teacher is not meant to be a teaching machine but a real human being. He/she must be someone who is kind, compassionate, friendly, available and approachable. He/she must show real warmth in his/her interactions with students. 2) He/She has to adopt a personal approach in his/her teaching. Just as good doctors do not just deal with the illness of a patient but rather treat a patient who is ill, so a good teacher does not teach some subjects, but rather teaches students. He/she looks upon them as real human persons who have come to the school to learn. 3) A good teacher must be able to take real interest in students as human beings and sincerely try to communicate to them his/her interest.

2. Our anonymous student makes some concrete suggestions about the method of teaching: "Help me to think, to learn and to judge for myself, not just memorize ready-made answers. Help me rather to find the answers myself, even though this way may be more painful for me".

   Here the student is suggesting that in the process of education he/she should not be looked upon as a passive recipient of the teacher's gift of knowledge, but as an active participant in the quest for knowledge. Many years ago Paulo Freire spoke of the 'banking concept of education' according to which the teacher 'deposits' knowledge in the minds of the students.[3] What takes place is a mere trasnferral of knowledge. The students do not perform acts of cognition. Teaching must be a process of empowering students. They have to be helped to learn how to learn. The teacher has to create conditions in which students experience the joy of search and the wonder of personal discovery. There is a Chinese proverb which says:

   Tell me, I shall forget
   Show me, I may remember
   Involve me, I will understand

3. The student now makes a request: "Do not expect of me what is beyond my talent or power".

   It is very important for a teacher to realize that his/her students are not equally gifted. Hence the teacher has to have a personalized approach to students. While it is necessary to challenge students to do their best, a teacher has to be patient and understanding towards weak students. An old teacher once remarked: I get my joy by teaching bright students; I earn my salary by teaching average students, and I win heaven by teaching dull students.

4. The student is aware of the need for some discipline: "Be strict will me provided that you are just. I know that I need it though outwardly I may rebel against it".

   I would like to make three comments on this suggestion of the student. 1. Some order is necessary in a classroom because it creates a climate of openness and discipline which makes teaching and learning easy. 2. Teachers should not unnecessarily curtail the freedom of students. For real learning takes place only in a relaxed atmosphere of freedom. 3. Most children are naturally good. If you have a sense of humour you can deal competently with the pranks of children. When a newly appointed teacher went to his class he saw on the blackboard written in bold letters: **Welcome to the**

Donkey. The teacher read it and was a bit confused. Then he regained his composure and wrote underneath: Mr. C. V. Jose. The children had a hearty laugh. That was the end of the whole affair.[4]

5. The student now makes an earnest request: "Listen seriously to the questions I may ask, however foolish they may sound to you".

   It is very important for the teacher to take every student and his/her questions seriously, He/she should not in any way ridicule a student whose questions may appear studpid. Every genuine question manifests the earnest quest of a young mind for clarity and certitude. Because of this the teacher should take his/her questions seriously and respond to them carefully.

6. Finally the student politely reminds the teacher that he has to be a constant learner: "Please keep studying yourself and do not mechanically use in the class the same yellow notes you wrote twenty years ago".

   We live in a world that is changing fast. In the world today there is an explosion of knowledge. In order to be a competent teacher in this time of change, a person has to be a continuous learner. Some years back a group of German university students wrote: Today we are being taught by teachers of yesterday according to the knowledge and methods of day before yesterday for our life tomorrow". I think that there is some truth in what these students are saying.

   Recently a suggestion has been mooted that universities should recall the degree conferred on a person if he/she has not updated himself/herself during the last five years. Maybe this suggestion should be taken seriously by the Vice-Chancellors of our universities.

   Thirty-seven years ago Pope John Paul II exhorted the Professors of the Gregorian University: "Strive to be constantly creative; do not be too easily satisfied with what was good enough for the past. Have the courage to be explore new paths…"[5]

   By way of conclusion I would like to request the teachers to bear in mind three things:

   1) The goal of education. It is significant that most of the leading educationists of all lands have believed the full flowering of the human on the earth to be the goal of education. A UNESCO study speaks of the development of the complete man or woman. "The physical, intellectual, emotional and ethical integration of the individual into a complete man or women is a broad definition of the fundamental aim for eduction. We find this a pedagogic ideal throughout history, in almost all countries, among philosophers and moralists, and among most theoreticians and visionaries of education. It has been one of the fundamental themes of humanist thought at all times. It may have been applied imperfectly, but it has been fruitful and helped to inspire many of the noblest educational enterprises."[6]

2) The danger of faulty education. Some years back a Headmaster wrote to every teacher of the school:

   Dear Teacher,

   I am a survivor of a concentration camp. My eyes saw what no man should witness:

   Gas chambers built by learned engineers. Children poisoned by educated physicians. Infants killed by trained nurses. Women and babies shot and burned by high school and college graduates.

   So, I am suspicious of education. My request: Help your students to become human. Your efforts must never produce learned monsters, skilled psychopaths, educated Eichmanns. Reading, writing, arithmetic are important only if they serve to make children more humane.[7]

3) The value of good education. Way back in 1966 the Kothari Commission on Education observed: "The destiny of India is now being shaped in her classrooms…" A few months before that Vatican II made this remarkable statement: "We can justly consider that the future of humanity lies in the hands of those who are strong enough to provide coming generations with reasons for living and hoping."[8]

   The teachers of today are called to render that service to the next generation.

Notes

1. C.P. Varkey, *Gently and Firmly*, Mumbai: St Pauls, 1995, p. 13.
2. As quoted by C. P. Varkey, *Gently and Firmly*, p. 13.
3. See Paulo Freire, *Pedagogy of the Oppressed*, London: Sheed and Ward, 1978, pp. 45–55.
4. As reported by C.P. Varkey, *Gently and Firmly*, p. 14.
5. Souvenir of the Pope's Visit: *John Paul II at the Gregorian University and the Biblical Institute, Rome,* 1979, p. 27.
6. E. Faure and Others, *Learning to Be*, Delhi, UNESCO, 1973, p. 156.
7. As quoted by C.P. Varkey, *Gently and Firmly*, pp. 19-20.
8. Vatican II, Pastoral Constitution on the Church in the Modern World, Rome, 1965, n. 31.

11

GROWTH IN THE CHURCH'S UNDERSTANDING OF MARRIAGE AND THE FAMILY

In 1965 Vatican II issued the Pastoral Constitution on the Church in the Modern World which has a chapter on the sacredness of Marriage and the Family. In many ways this chapter marks the beginning of a new approach to marriage and the family. In 1981 Pope John Paul II published the Apostolic Exhortation, *Familiaris Consortio,* which adopts the new approach of Vatican II and develops it further. In 2015 Pope Francis issued the Apostolic Exhortation, *Amoris Laetitia* (The Joy of Love), which takes further steps in the articulation of a new understanding of marriage and the family in continuity with the Pastoral Constitution and the Apostolic Exhortation of John Paul II.

In this chapter I shall contend that this is a clear case of doctrinal development. But in order to grasp the newness of the Church's teaching on marriage and the family during the last fifty years we must examine the Church's understanding of marriage and the family before Vatican II.

This chapter is divided into four parts. Part one describes the Church's understanding of marriage and the family before Vatican II. Part two analyses the chapter in the Pastoral Constitution on the sacredness of marriage and the family. Part three deals with the Apostolic Exhortation of John Paul II. Part four examines the teaching of *Amoris Laetitia.*

Part I. Before Vatican II

In this period the documents of the Church only discuss marriage. Though they speak of children there is hardly any mention of family life. Here is a brief summary of the Church's teaching on marriage before Vatican II.

1. The Church powerfully affirms the goodness of marriage against those who tended to deny it. In the history of the Church the Manichaeans, the Priscillianists, the Waldenses and some others contended that there were two

kingdoms: 1. The kingdom of spirit and light which was created by God; 2. The kingdom of matter and darkness which was created by the devil. Because of this view they despised the material world, the human body, sex and marriage. Against them the Church clearly asserted that God is the Creator of all things, both spiritual and material, visible and invisible. It forcefully condemned all those who denied that marriage was a true human value. Already in 561 AD, the Council of Braga rejected the teachings of Manichaeans and the Priscillianists:

If anyone condemns human marriage and despises *(perhorrescit)* the procreation of children, as Manes and Priscillian have said, *anathema sit.*

If anyone says that the formation of the human body is the work of the devil and that the conception of children in their mothers' womb is brought about through the activity of the devil, and for this reason does not believe in the resurrection of the body, as Manes and Priscillian have said, *anathema sit.*[1]

2. Marriage is a contract established by the consent of the partners. In answer to an inquiry made by the emperor of the Bulgarians, who were recently converted to Christianity, as regards the essence of Christian marriage, Pope Nicholas, in a letter to the Bulgarians (866 AD), declared that the consent of the partners is as in Roman law the essential element of Christian marriage.[2] In this context the pope quotes John Chrysostom's words: "It is not coitus but will that makes marriage."[3] But in early Middle Ages a controversy arose about the sufficiency of the consent of the partners for a valid marriage. Some people basing themselves on German law held that the conjugal act is necessary for a marriage to be valid. Others under the leadership of Peter Lombard maintained the tradition that the consent of the partners is sufficient. Pope Alexander III settled the issue by declaring that mutual consent makes the marriage, but the bond is perfected and becomes absolutely indissoluble through consummation.

3. Marriage is a Sacrament. Already in 1439 the Council of Florence in its Decree for the Armenians stated: "The seventh is the sacrament of matrimony which is the sign of the union of Christ and the Church according to the saying of the apostle: This is a great mystery and I am applying it to Christ and the Church", (Eph 5:32).[4]

The Council of Trent powerfully asserted the sacramentality of marriage against the Reformers who denied it. It declared that matrimony is "truly and properly one of the seven sacraments instituted by Christ the Lord."[5] Trent defends monogamy and affirms the indissolubility of the marriage bond. It vindicates the Church's authority to legislate on the marriage of Catholics.[6]

4. The Council of Florence teaches that the first aim of marriage is the begetting and the education of children.[7] Pius XI holds that marriage as an institution is destined for the procreation and education of children.[8]
5. Pope Leo XIII strongly opposed the attempt by the supporters of the civil power to separate the marriage contract from the sacrament. He taught "that in Christian marriage the contract cannot be dissociated from the sacrament; thus there can be no legitimate contract which is not also a sacrament. For Christ the Lord raised matrimony to the dignity of a sacrament, and matrimony is the contract itself provided it is legally made."[9]
6. Pius XI speaks of fidelity in marriage, "that is, the mutual faithfulness of husband and wife in observing the marital pledge. This implies that the right, which in virtue of the divinely ratified agreement belongs to each spouse, will neither be denied to the other nor be granted to any third party."[10]
7. Pope Leo XIII has stated that, by virtue of the sacrament of matrimony, "the spouses, sheltered and strengthened by the grace which his (Christ's) merits have won, should attain sanctification in marriage itself."[11] And Pius XI adds that the sacrament of matrimony confers on the spouses sanctifying grace which is the permanent principle of supernatural life; "it also gives them the right to obtain the help of actual grace whenever they need it for the discharge of their duties belonging to the married state.[12]
8. How have moral theologians before Vatican II understood marriage?

   In his book, *Moral Theology*, written in 1951, and translated into English by Fr Urban Adelmen in 1962, Fr Heribert Jone gives a brief definition of marriage:

   The marriage contract is a contract by which two competent persons of opposite sex give to each other the exclusive and irrevocable right over their bodies (*ius in corpus*) for the procreation and education of children.[13]

   There are three points noticeable in this definition. 1. Marriage is a contract. 2. The object of the contract are the bodies of the partners. They surrender their bodies to each other. 3. The purpose of this surrender of their bodies is the procreation and education of Children.

   In 1963 two respected moralists clarified the relationship between the various ends of marriage: If we look at marriage as a natural and divine institution, then in the intention of God and nature procreation is seen to be an end of greater importance or greater value than mutual help, conjugal love, and the remedy for concupiscence. Undoubtedly procreation and rearing of children are of more importance to the species. Likewise it is of more importance to human society in general, and hence to the law, both civil and canon. One must therefore, for valid philosophical reasons, call procreation primary. Since the *good of the species* is more important to nature than the good of individuals, procreation and rearing of children is a more important end of marriage than mutual help, conjugal love and the remedy.[14]

II. The Teaching of Vatican II on Marriage and the Family

2.1 Preliminary remarks

It is in the Pastoral Constitution on the Church in the Modern World, Part II, chapter one, that the Council articulates its understanding of marriage and the family. This chapter has to be read and interpreted in the light of what Vatican II has taught in the whole Constitution. As Bernard Häring has pointed out: "It is of decisive importance that the various statements of the chapter on marriage and the family are always envisaged and interpreted in the perspective of the Constitution as a whole."[15] Besides, we need to keep in mind what the Constitution has said in Part I about the dignity and freedom of the human person, "its irreplaceable uniqueness and its essentially social vocation which extends to the whole world." It is also said that the point of view of "the gospel" and human experience have to be combined. It seems to be clear that gospel here does not mean the various statements found in it, but rather "a light in which human experience finds its true meaning."

The chapter begins with a brief examination of the actual situation of marriage and the family in the modern world. There are both positive and negative elements in the situation.[16]

There is a growing awareness among people that the well-being of individual persons and that of human and Christian society is closely bound up with the healthy state of marriage and the family. Christians and all those who esteem conjugal and family life are happy to notice the different ways in which progress is being made in promoting the partnership of love and in encouraging reverence for human life. It is significant that more and more services are made available to married couples and parents for fulfilling their lofty calling. And there is hope of more benefits accruing to them and serious efforts are being made to bring them about.

However, this happy picture of married life is not found everywhere. There are factors which have a negative impact on marriage and the family – polygamy, the plague of divorce, so-called free love and similar things. Besides, marital love is often harmed by selfishness, hedonism and unlawful contraceptive practices. Moreover, the atmosphere in society is vitiated by social, economic, psychological, and civil factors which seriously disturb family life. In many parts of the world population explosion is causing alarming problems. Because of all this the conscience of many people are disturbed.

And yet, the beauty and vigour of the institution of marriage and the family shine forth time and again. In spite of all the hardships flowing from the fast changing conditions of society today, the real nature of marriage and the family is somehow revealed.

In the hope of guiding and encouraging Christians and all humans who are trying to preserve and promote the dignity and supremely sacred value of married life, the Council seeks to spell out clearly certain key points of the Church's teaching on marriage and the family.

There are two parts of Vatican II teaching on marriage and the family.

A. Vatican II accepts the following from tradition:

1. The divine origin of marriage. This is the way it expresses it: "God himself is the author of matrimony and endowed as it is with various benefits and purposes." Marriage "has been established by the Creator and qualified by His laws."
2. Christ has raised marriage to the dignity of a sacrament.[17]
3. The indissolubility of marriage. The intimate union of the spouses imposes total and perpetual fidelity on them and "argues for an unbreakable oneness."[18]

B. However, Vatican II has quite a new way of understanding marriage and the family.

1. "Marriage is an intimate partnership of life and love... It is rooted in the covenant of irrevocable personal consent."[19] Vatican II does not consider marriage a contract between a man and a woman.
2. The Council has a new and inspiring understanding of conjugal love. It spells out its understanding thus:
   - "This love is an eminently human one since it is directed from one person to another and involves the good of the whole person."[20]
   - "Such love, merging the human with the divine, leads the spouses to a free and mutual gift of themselves, a gift proving itself by gentle affection and by deed. Such love persuades the whole of their lives"[21]
   - "This love is uniquely expressed and perfected through the marital act. The actions within marriage by which the couple are united intimately and chastely are noble and worthy ones."[22]
3. Vatican II has a new way of understanding the sacrament of matrimony: The Saviour of humankind and "the spouse of the Church comes into the lives of married Christians through the sacrament of matrimony. He abides with them thereafter so that, just as he loved the Church and handed himself over on her behalf, the spouses may love each other with perpetual fidelity through mutual self-bestowal."[23]
4. Vatican II rejects the traditional distinction between the primary and the secondary ends of marriage. And yet it declares:

   Marriage and conjugal love are by their nature ordained toward the begetting and educating of children.[24]

   Still the Council maintains that marriage as a whole manner and communion of life remains valid even when the couple cannot have children. The reason for this is that marriage is not instituted solely for procreation, but that the mutual love of the spouses may be expressed in an orderly manner, that it grow and ripen.[25]

5. The Council was seriously concerned about respect for human life. Hence it exhorts the couples:

   For God, the Lord of life, has conferred on human beings the surpassing ministry of safeguarding life - a ministry which must be fulfilled in a manner which is worthy of the human person. Therefore from the moment of its conception life must be guarded with the greatest care, while abortion and infanticide are unspeakable crimes. The sexual characteristics of the human person and the human faculty of reproduction wonderfully exceed the dispositions of lower forms of life. Hence the acts themselves which are proper to conjugal love and which are exercised in accord with genuine human dignity must be honoured with great reverence.[26]

6. Children are in a true sense the supreme gift of marriage and contribute substantially to the welfare of their parents. God in his goodness has chosen to share with parents a participation in his creative work. As Vatican II clarifies:

   Hence, while not making the other purposes of matrimony of less account, the true practice of conjugal love, and the whole meaning of the family life which results from it, have this aim: that the couple be ready with stout hearts to cooperate with the love of the Creator and the Saviour, who through them will enlarge and enrich His own family day by day.[27]

7. Because of a variety of reasons parents may have to practise responsible parenthood. While they plan to limit the number of children they will have, parents have to take into account several factors. They should think of their own welfare and that of the children they already have. They should be concerned about the material and spiritual conditions of the times. They have to take note of the interests of the state and the Church. As the Council clearly states:

   The parents themselves should ultimately make this judgment in the sight of God. But in their manner of acting spouses should be aware that they cannot proceed arbitrarily. They must always be governed according to a conscience dutifully conformed to the divine law itself, and should be submissive toward the Church's teaching office, which authentically interprets that law in the light of the gospel. That divine law reveals and protects the integral meaning of conjugal love, and impels it toward a truly human fulfilment.[28]

   Vatican II reminds people that human life and the task of transmitting it are realities that have a bearing not only on our life here on earth but also on the eternal destiny of human beings.[29]

8. Children are the fruit of marriage. As Vatican II emphatically states:
Parents should regard as their proper mission the task of transmitting human life and educating those to whom it has been transmitted. They should realize that they are thereby cooperators with the love of God the Creator, and are, so to speak, the interpreters of that love. Thus they will fulfil the task with human and Christian responsibility.[30]
Education of their children is a serious responsibility of the parents. As the Council observes:
As a result, with their parents leading the way by example and family prayer, children and indeed everyone gathered around the family hearth will find a readier path to human maturity, salvation, and holiness. Graced with the dignity and office of fatherhood and motherhood, parents will energetically acquit themselves of a duty which devolves primarily on them, namely education, and especially religious education.[31]
Vatican II makes two important observations about the education of children:

1) The family is a kind of school of deeper humanity. In order to achieve the full flowering of its life and mission parents need to cooperate wholeheartedly in the education of their children.
The active presence of the father is highly beneficial to their formation. The children, especially the younger among them, need the care of their mother at home. This domestic role of hers must be safely preserved, though the legitimate social progress of women should not be underrated on that account.[32]
2) Parents have to educate children in such a way that they are prepared for adult life. This will enable children, when they become adults, to follow their vocation, including a religious one and choose a state of life.[33]
Parents or guardians should by prudent advice provide guidance to their young with respect to founding a family, and the young ought to listen gladly. At the same time no pressure, direct or indirect, should be put on the young to make them enter marriage or choose a specific partner.[34]

9. Children can make a contribution to the happiness of their parents and their growth in holiness. In the words of the Council:
As living members of the family, children contribute in their own way to making their parents holy. For they will respond to the kindness of their parents with sentiments of gratitude, with love and trust. They will stand by them as children should when hardships overtake their parents and old age brings its loneliness.[35]

Since the family is the foundation of Society and all those concerned about the welfare of the Society have to promote the good estate of marriage and the family: community leaders, public authorities and fellow Christians.[36]

10. But priests have a significant role to play. They have to get trained in family matters. Then they will be able to nurture the vocation of the spouses by a variety of pastoral helps – by preaching the word, by liturgical worship and by other spiritual aids to conjugal and family life. They should stand by them sympathetically and patiently when couples and members of the family are passing through difficult times. They should enable them to become courageous through love.[37]

To sum up:

Thus the Christian family, which springs from marriage as a reflection of the loving covenant uniting Christ with the Church, and as a participation in that covenant, will manifest to all human beings the Saviour's living presence in the world, and the genuine nature of the Church. This the family will do by the mutual love of the spouses, by their generous fruitfulness, their solidarity and faithfulness, and by the loving way in which all members of the family work together.[38]

III. The Teaching of *Familiarins Consortio*

In November 1981 Pope John Paul II issued an Apostolic Exhortation, titled *Familiaris Consortio*, on the role of the Christian family in the modern world. This Exhortation is based on the Synod of Bishops, held in Rome from September 26 to October 25, 1980. As the Pope made it clear:

At the close of their assembly, the Synod Fathers presented me with a long list of proposals in which they had gathered the fruits of their reflections, which had matured over intense days of work, and they asked me unanimously to be a spokesman before humanity of the Church's lively care for the family and to give suitable indications for renewed pastoral effort in this fundamental sector of the life of man and of the Church.[39]

On a careful examination of the Exhortation it has become clear to me that it basically agrees with the understanding of marriage and the family found in the Pastoral Constitution of the Church in the Modern World of Vatican II. But it articulates its position in a nuanced way. There are two parts to its teaching.

A. The Exhortation agrees with Vatican II in the following points.

1. Marriage and family are willed by God in the very act of creation.[40] The intimate community of life and love shaped by the covenant of conjugal love freely and consciously chosen by a man and a woman is willed by God. As a result "their bond of love becomes the image and symbol of the covenant which unites God and His people". In other words, the communion of love

between God and people… finds a meaningful expression in the covenant which is established between a man and woman.[41]

2. Jesus Christ reveals the original truth of marriage, the truth of the beginning, and, freeing human beings from their hardness of heart, he makes them capable of realizing this truth in its entirety. As the Exhortation points out: This revelation reaches its definitive fullness in the gift of love which the Word of God makes to humanity in assuming a human nature, and in the sacrifice which Jesus Christ makes of Himself on the Cross for His bride, the Church. In this sacrifice there is entirely revealed that plan which God has imprinted on the humanity of man and woman since their creation; the marriage of baptized persons thus becomes a real symbol of that new and eternal covenant sanctioned in the blood of Christ."[42]

   Hence, the marriage of the baptized is one of the seven sacraments of the New Covenant. "By the sacramentality of their marriage, spouses are bound to one another in the most profoundly indissoluble manner. Their belonging to each other is the real representation, by means of the sacramental sign, of the very relationship of Christ with the Church".[43] As Pope John Paul II clarifies: "The first and immediate effect of marriage (*res et sacramentum*)" is not supernatural grace itself, but the Christian conjugal bond, a typically Christian communion of two persons, because it represents the mystery of Christ's incarnation and the mystery of His covenant."[44]

3. Love is the basis of both marriage and the family. As the Exhortation states: God is love and in Himself he lives a mystery of personal loving communion. Creating the human race in Hs own image and continually keeping it in being, God inscribed in the humanity of man and woman the vocation, and thus the capacity and responsibility, of love and communion. Love is therefore the fundamental and innate vocation of every human being.[45]

   Since the human being is an incarnate spirit he/she is called to love in a unified totality. "Love includes the body, and the body is made a sharer in spiritual love". As the Exhortation remarks: "Consequently, sexuality, by means of which man and woman give themselves to one another through the acts which are proper and exclusive to spouses, is by no means something purely biological, but concerns the innermost being of the human person as such. It is realized in a truly human way only if it is an integral part of the love by which a man and a woman commit themselves totally to one another until death."[46]

4. The Exhortation strongly affirms the equal dignity of man and woman. It quotes with approval those memorable words of Vatican II: "Firmly established by the Lord, the unity of marriage will radiate the equal personal dignity of husband and wife, a dignity acknowledged by mutual and total love."[47]

Above all it is important to underline the equal dignity and responsibility of women with men. This equality is realized in a unique manner in that reciprocal self-giving by each one to the other and by both to the children which is proper to marriage and the family.[48]

5. Together with Vatican II the Apostolic Exhortation declares that "the institution of marriage and conjugal love are ordained to the procreation and education of children in whom they find their crowning."[49] It goes on to add: In its most profound reality, love is essentially a gift; and conjugal love, while leading the spouses to the reciprocal "knowledge which makes them "one flesh," does not end with couple, because it makes them capable of the greatest possible gift: a person. Thus the couple, while giving themselves to one another, give not just themselves but also the reality of children, who are a living reflection of their being a father and a mother.[50]

   In this context the Exhortation clarifies two questions: 1) It does not make the other purposes of marriage of less value, when it emphatically states that the practice of conjugal love has this aim: "that the couple be ready with stout hearts to cooperate with the love of the Creator and Saviour, who through them will enlarge and enrich his own family day by day; 2) Even when procreation is not possible, conjugal love and marriage do not for this reason lose their value.

6. Basing itself on Vatican II and Paul VI, the exhortation insists that the "love between husband and wife must be fully human, exclusive and open to new life."[51] In this connection it appeals to Paul VI to show that the Church's teaching on marriage and the generation and education of children is supported by an integral vision of the human person.

   It is precisely by moving from "an integral vision of man and of his vocation, not only his natural and earthly, but also his supernatural and eternal vocation, that Paul VI affirmed that the teaching of the Church "is founded upon the inseparable connection, willed by God and unable to be broken by man on his own initiative, between the two meanings of the conjugal act: the unitive meaning and the procreative meaning". And he concluded by re-emphasizing that there must be excluded as intrinsically immoral "every action which, either in anticipation of the conjugal act, or in its accomplishment, or in the development of its natural consequences, proposes, whether as an end or as a means, to render procreation impossible."[52]

7. The Apostolic Exhortation powerfully affirms the indissolubility of marriage:

   Conjugal communion is characterized not only by its unity but also by its indissolubility: "As a mutual gift to two persons, this intimate

union, as well as the good of children, imposes total fidelity on the spouses and argues for an unbreakable oneness between them.[53]
Being rooted in the personal and total self-giving of the couple, and being required by the good of the children, the indissolubility of marriage finds its ultimate truth in the plan that God has manifested in His revelation: He wills and He communicates the indissolubility of marriage as a fruit, a sign and a requirement of the absolutely faithful love the God has for man and that the Lord Jesus has for the Church.[54]
The Exhortation reminds Christian couples that they "are called to participate in the irrevocable indissolubility that binds Christ to His Church, His bride."[55]

8. The parents have the right and the duty to educate their children. As the Exhortation explains: "The task of giving education is rooted in the primary vocation of married couples to participate in God's creative activity: by begetting in love and for love a new person who has within himself or herself the vocation to growth and development, parents by that very fact take on the task of helping that person effectively to live a fully human life."[56]
9. Children and parents promote the growth of each other:
A fundamental opportunity for building such a communion is constituted by the educational exchange between parents and children, in which each gives and receives. By means of love, respect and obedience towards their parents, children offer their specific and irreplaceable contribution to the construction of an authentically human and Christian family.[57]
The family, which is founded and given life by love, is a community of persons: of husband and wife, of parents and children, of relatives. Its first task is to live with fidelity the reality of communion in a constant effort to develop an authentic community of persons.[58]

B. The Contribution of *Familaris Consortio*

While we do not find any new ideas about the nature of marriage and the family in John Paul II's Apostolic Exhortation, *Familiaris Consortio*, it has given us several valuable insights. I shall now highlight some of them.

1. The intimate relationship between the human being and love: "Man cannot live without love. He remains a being that is incomprehensible for himself, his life is senseless, if love is not revealed to him, if he does not encounter love, if he does not encounter it and make it his own, if he does not participate intimately in it."[59]
2. The Exhortation points out that the institution of matrimony should not be regarded as an undue interference by society or an extrinsic imposition of a form. It is rather an interior requirement of the covenant of conjugal

love which is professed as unique and exclusive in order to live in complete fidelity to the plan of God, the Creator. A person's freedom far from being restricted by this fidelity is secured against every form of subjectivism or relativism and is made a sharer in creative Wisdom."[60]

3. The Exhortation recognizes the right and the duty of couples to transmit life in a responsible way. For the Church is aware of "the serious problem of population growth in the form it has taken in the many parts of the world". The document is clearly against the use of artificial means of birth-control. But it is in favour of periodic continence as method of a regulating birth: When, instead, by means of recourse to periods of infertility, the couple respect the inseparable connection between the unitive and procreative meanings of human sexuality, they are acting as "ministers" of God's plan and they "benefit from" their sexuality according to the original dynamism of "total" self-giving, without manipulation or alteration.[61]
   It goes on to add:

   > To accept the cycle and to enter into dialogue means to recognize both the spiritual and corporal character of conjugal communion and to live personal love with its requirement of fidelity. In this context the couple comes to experience how conjugal communion is enriched with those values of tenderness and affection which constitute the inner soul of human sexuality, in its physical dimension also. In this way sexuality is respected and promoted in its truly and fully human dimension, and is never "used" as an "object" that, by breaking the personal unity of soul and body, strikes at God's creation itself at the level of the deepest interaction of nature and person.[62]

   1) In this connection the Exhortation makes two important points: 1) It clarifies why the Church condemns all those who would force couples to adopt artificial means of birth-control:
      Thus the Church condemns as a grave offense against human dignity and justice all those activities of governments or other public authorities which attempt to limit in any way the freedom of couples in deciding about children. Consequently, any violence applied by such authorities in favour of contraception or, still worse, of sterilization and procured abortion, must be altogether condemned and forcefully rejected. Likewise to be denounced as gravely unjust are cases where, in international relations, economic help given for the advancement of peoples is made conditional on programmes of contraception, sterilization and procured abortion.[63]
   2) The Exhortation asks experts to make available to people at large a clear knowledge about the bodily aspect and the body's rhythms of fertility:

Accordingly, every effort must be made to render such knowledge accessible to all married people and also to young adults before marriage, through clear, timely and serious instruction and education given by married couples, doctors and experts. Knowledge must then lead to education in self-control: hence the absolute necessity for the virtue of chastity and for permanent education in it. In the Christian view, chastity by no means signifies rejection of human sexuality or lack of esteem for it: rather it signifies spiritual energy capable of defending love from the perils of selfishness and aggressiveness, and able to advance it towards its full realization:[64]

The document also asks theologians to support the Church's authentic teaching on birth regulation as proposed in the Second Vatican Council and in the Encyclical *Humanae Vitae*:

For this reason, together with the Synod Fathers I feel it is my duty to extend a pressing invitation to theologians, asking them to unite their efforts in order to collaborate with the hierarchical Magisterium and to commit themselves to the task of illustrating ever more clearly the biblical foundations, the ethical grounds and the personalistic reasons behind this doctrine. Thus it will be possible, in the context of an organic exposition, to render the teaching of the Church on this fundamental question truly accessible to all people of good will, fostering a daily more enlightened and profound understanding of it: in this way God's plan will be ever more completely fulfilled for the salvation of humanity and for the glory of the Creator.[65]

4. The valuable contribution that the family makes to society. The deep experience of communion and sharing in the family's daily life represents its first and fundamental contribution to society. Family is the place of origin and the most effective means for humanizing and personalizing society. This is very important in our time when society is runs the risk of becoming more and more depersonalized.[66]

   Besides, families can either singly or association devote themselves to a variety of social service activities, especially in favour of the poor.
5. The family participates in the life and mission of the Church. Since it is a domestic church, a Church in miniature, it is a "living image and historical representation of the mystery of the Church". The Christian family is called upon to take part actively in the mission of the Church. It also helps to build up the kingdom of God.[67]
6. Christian couples and parents can make a significant contribution to the Church's evangelical discernment in different situations and cultures in which men and women live their marriage and family life. "They are qualified for this role by the gift of the sacrament of matrimony."[68]

IV. The Teaching of *Amoris Laetitia*

On March 19, 2016, Pope Francis issued an Apostolic Exhortation, titled *Amoris Laetitia*, on love in the Family. This Exhortation is largely based on the findings of two synods of Bishops held in Rome in 2014 and 2015. As the Pope has stated:

For this reason, I thought it appropriate to prepare a post-synodal Apostolic Exhortation to gather the contributions of the two recent Synods on the family, while adding other considerations as an aid to reflection, dialogue and pastoral practice, and as a help and encouragement to families in their daily commitments and challenges.[69]

The Exhortation largely agrees with the Pastoral Constitution on the Church on the Church in the Modern world of Vatican II and the Apostolic Exhortation *Familiaris Consortio* of John Paul II. It also contains valuable insights of its own.

A. These are the points of agreement:

1. God is the author of marriage. *Amoris Laetitia* formulates this idea in its own way: "Marriage is a gift from the Lord."[70] The exhortation speaks of God's original plan for man and woman. It "emphasizes the need to safeguard God's gift". Finally, "the mystery of the Christian family can be fully understood only in the light of the Father's infinite love revealed in Christ."[71]
2. Marriage is a partnership of life and love.[72] Marriage is founded on the mutual love of man and woman.
3. Marriage is not a contract but a covenant. *Amoris Laetitia* speaks of the "words of consent in which the couple accepted and offered themselves each to the other. Their conjugal love leads the partners to a free and mutual self-giving.[73]
4. Marriage is also a sacrament. "The sacrament of marriage is not a social convention, an empty ritual or merely the outward sign of a commitment. The sacrament is a gift given for the sanctification and salvation of the spouses."[74] The love between the husband and wife "is sanctified, enriched and illuminated by the grace of the sacrament of marriage."[75]
5. The indissolubility of Marriage. After describing the traits of the friendship between the spouses *Amoris Laetitia* adds: "Marriage joins to all this an indissoluble exclusivity expressed in the stable commitment to share and shape together the whole of life."[76] Pope Francis states that the "Synod Fathers noted that Jesus in speaking of God's original plan for man and woman reaffirmed the indissoluble union between them."[77] He goes on to add: The indissolubility of marriage…should not be viewed as a yoke imposed on humanity, but as a gift granted to those who are joined in marriage."[78]
6. According to the order of creation conjugal love between a man and a woman and the transmission of life are ordered to each other. Thus God

made man and woman share in the work of creation."[79] *Amoris Laetitia* adds: "The child who is born does not come from outside as something added on to the mutual love of the spouses, but springs from the very heart of that mutual giving, as it fruit and fulfilment."[80]

The Exhortation quotes with approval the significant statement of Vatican II: "Marriage was not instituted solely for the procreation of Children, but also that mutual love might be properly expressed, that it should grow and mature."[81] Hence, marriage is perfectly valid even when the couple cannot have children.

7. *Amoris Laetitia* strongly supports responsible parenthood. Quoting Pope John Paul II, it explains "that responsible parenthood does not mean unlimited procreation or lack of awareness of what is involved in rearing children, but rather the empowerment of couples to use their invaluable liberty wisely and responsibly, taking into account social and demographic realities, as well as their own situation and legitimate desires."[82]
8. Parents are the primary educators of their children. Other people and other agencies can help the parents in this noble task, but they cannot replace them. "They should take up this essential role and carry it out consciously, enthusiastically, reasonably and appropriately."[83]

B. The Contribution of *Amoris Laetitia*

1. Pope Francis interprets Paul's hymn to love in 1 Corinthians 13 in such way that it becomes relevant and meaningful to the life of the couples and their families.[84]
2. The Pope calls attention to the reality of violence and manipulation in married life.

   In his opinion "sex often becomes depersonalized and unhealthy; as a result it becomes an occasion and instrument for self-assertion and the selfish satisfaction of personal desires and instincts. In our own day, sexuality risks bring poisoned by the mentality of "use and discard."[85]
3. Pope Francis believes that virginity and marriage are two ways of living a life of love, but one is not better than the other. As he points out: "Whereas virginity is an 'eschatological' sign of the risen Christ, marriage is a 'historical' sign for us living in this world, a sign of the earthly Christ who chose to become one of us and gave himself up for us even shedding his blood. Virginity and marriage are, and must be, different ways of loving."[86]
4. Pope Francis believes that the moral formation of children is the responsibility of parents. They can rely on schools to ensure the basic instruction of their children, but not for their moral formation. "Parents are also responsible for shaping the will of their children, fostering good habits and a natural inclination to goodness. This entails presenting certain ways of thinking and acting as desirable and worthwhile, as part of a gradual process of growth.

The desire to fit into society, or the habit of foregoing an immediate pleasure for the sake of a better and more orderly life in common, is itself a value that can then inspire openness to greater values."[87]

Pope Francis is of the opinion that moral formation should make use of active methods and should be in a language that children can understand.

5. The Pope has strongly advocated a helpful pastoral approach to people in difficult marriage situations. They may be divorced persons or those who are divorced and remarried. They may be people involved in civil marriages or those who are just cohabiting.

Objectively speaking these people may be in sinful situations, but there are factors that mitigate their subjective guilt. In this connection Pope Francis quotes with approval The Catechism of the Catholic Church:

Imputability and responsibility for an action can be diminished or even nullified by ignorance, inadvertence, duress, fear, habit, inordinate attachments, and other psychological or social factors."[88] In another paragraph, the Catechism refers once again to circumstances which mitigate moral responsibility, and mentions at length "affective immaturity, force of acquired habit, conditions of anxiety or other psychological or social factors that lesson or even extenuate moral culpability."[89]

Hence pastors should not rush into judgement of the guilt of people in difficult marriage situations. They have to remember that "under certain circumstances people find it very difficult to act differently."[90]

Besides, pastors should embody the mercy and compassion of Jesus Christ in their attitude and behavior.

By way of conclusion I wish to make three points:

1) Vatican II has articulated a radically new understanding of marriage and the family. For me this is a clear case of doctrinal development.
2) The Apostolic Exhortation *Familiaris Consortio* of John Paul II and the Apostolic Exhortation *Amoris Laetitia* of Pope Francis have reinforced the teaching of Vatican II.
3) The Pastoral Constitution on the Church in the Modern World of Vatican II and the Apostolic Exhortations of Pope John Paul II and Pope Francis have elaborated a new and helpful pastoral approach to married people and their family, especially to those in difficult marriage situations. These documents have also clarified the role of the Christian families in the Church and in secular society.

Notes

1. J. Neuner-J. Dupuis, *The Christian Faith*, Bangalore: TPI, 2008, n.n. 402/11-12
2. J Neuner-Dupuis, *The Christian Faith*, n. 1801
3. J Chrysostom, *Opus Imperfectum in Matthaeum,* Hom. 32,9.
4. J. Neuner J Dupuis, *The Christian Faith*, n. 1803
5. Ibid. n. 1808

6. Ibid. n. 1809, 1811
7. Ibid. n. 1808
8. Ibid. n. 1822
9. Ibid. n. 1828
10. Ibid. n. 1820
11. Ibid. n. 1832
12. Ibid.
13. H. Jone, *Moral Theology*, Maryland: The Newman Press, 1962, p. 656
14. J. C. Ford and G. Kelley, *Contemporary Moral Theology*, Vol. Two, Westminster, Maryland: The Newman Press, 1963, p. 130
15. B. Harling, "Commentary on the Pastoral Constitution on the Church in the Modern World, Part II, Chapter I" in H. Vorgrimier, *Commentary on the Documents of Vatican II*, Vol. 5, New York: Herder, 1969, p. 228.
16. Pastoral Constitution on the Church in the Modern World, Rome (GS) 1965. N. 47.
17. Ibid. n. 48
18. Ibid.
19. Ibid.
20. *Ibid.* n. 49
21. Ibid.
22. Ibid.
23. *Ibid.* n. 48
24. Ibid. n. 50
25. Ibid.
26. Ibid. n. 51
27. Ibid. n. 50
28. Ibid.
29. Ibid.
30. Ibid. n. 48
31. Ibid. n. 52
32. Ibid.
33. Ibid.
34. Ibid. n. 48.
35. Ibid.
36. Ibid. n. 52
37. Ibid.
38. Ibid. n. 48
39. John Paul II, Familiaris Consortio, Rome, 1981, n. 2
40. Ibid. n. 3
41. Ibid. n. 12
42. Ibid. n. 13
43. Ibid.
44. Ibid.
45. Ibid. n. 11
46. Ibid.
47. Ibid. n. 19
48. Ibid. n. 22
49. Ibid. n. 14
50. Ibid.
51. Ibid. n. 29
52. Ibid. n. 32

53. Ibid. n. 20
54. Ibid.
55. Ibid.
56. Ibid. n. 36
57. Ibid. n. 21
58. Ibid. n. 18
59. Ibid.
60. Ibid. n. 11
61. Ibid. n. 32
62. Ibid.
63. Ibid. n. 30
64. Ibid. n. 33
65. Ibid. n. 31
66. Ibid. n. 43
67. Ibid. n. 52
68. Ibid. n. 54
69. Amoris Laetitia, n. 4
70. AL n. 61
71. AL n. 59
72. AL n. 67
73. AL n. 76
74. AL n. 72
75. AL n. 120
76. AL n. 123
77. AL n. 62
78. Ibid.
79. AL n. 80
80. Ibid.
81. AL n. 125
82. AL n. 167
83. AL n. 259
84. See AL n.n. 91-119
85. AL n. 153
86. AL n. 161
87. AL n. 264
88. AL n. 302
89. Ibid.
90. Ibid.

12

THE CHALLENGE OF MARTIN LUTHER'S REFORMATION

The Response of Vatican II

The beginnings of Martin Luther's reformation can be traced back to October 31, 1517. On that day Luther posted his 95 theses on the door of the castle church in Wittenberg, Germany. In those days it was common practice among professors to post their theses in public places as an invitation to debate.

What is remarkable about Luther's 95 Theses is that they make a radical critique of the practice of indulgence sale authorized by the Pope. As Paul W. Robinson has observed:

> Although the theses tend to defy a simple analysis, three broad categories of Luther's concern can be identified. The theses express, first of all, Luther's understanding of penance as it relates to indulgences. The very first states, "When our Lord and Master Jesus Christ said, 'Repent,' he willed the entire life of the believer to be one of repentance." As Luther explained in the second thesis, the repentance Christ preached meant much more than doing the penances assigned by the priest... For Luther, indulgences fostered a mechanical understanding of repentance that undermined the biblical teaching... Second, Luther called into question the belief that indulgences could be purchased on behalf of a soul in purgatory, freeing that soul to enter heaven. This common belief preached by Tetzel, "When the coin in the coffer rings, the soul from purgatory springs," which Luther quoted in Thesis 27, became the object of his scorn in Thesis 28: "It is certain that when money clinks in the money chest, greed and avarice can be increased." The observation about souls in purgatory led Luther

> to put forth a more restrictive view of the pope's power… Thesis 5: "The pope neither desires nor is able to remit any penalties except those imposed by his own authority or that of the canons." and that, in any case, souls in purgatory were beyond his jurisdiction… Third, Luther described indulgences, or at least trust in them, as detrimental to genuine Christian living. He would rather see the money used for indulgences spent on the poor and the time people spent in acquiring indulgences spent in prayer instead… Thesis 48: "Christians are to be taught that the pope… needs and thus desires their devout prayer more than their money."[1]

From these small beginnings Luther's efforts grew into a radical reform movement.

The Council of Trent (1545-1563) discussed the main points of Luther's Reformation and articulated a Catholic response to his questions. Looking back on that council and its decrees one wonders if the council Fathers really tried to understand Luther sympathetically and respond to him constructively. Today the acts of Trent appear to be quite one-sided and reactionary. It was a critical time when the very existence of Catholicism was seriously threatened.[2] Hence the council of Trent was primarily concerned about defending the Church and its essential teaching. It had no time and interest in understanding Luther's genuine concern for the reform of the Church.

It was probably Vatican II that constructively responded to the challenge of Luther's Reformation. In this paper I shall discuss the main challenges of Luther's Reformation and explain the response of Vatican II.

1. The Challenge to Church Authority

There are four points in Luther's position on Church authority:

1. The Pope has no spiritual authority, but only secular authority. In Luther's time "the pope functioned and was treated as another secular ruler"[3], the ruler of the papal states. Many German Catholics were of the same opinion as Luther.
2. Luther denied that the Pope has authority by divine right. As Paul W. Robinson has observed:

> Luther asserted (during his disputation will Johann Eck at Leipzik in 1519) that the Pope had his authority by human arrangement rather than by divine right. He did not yet argue against the pope's authority or against the need for unity in the Church, but he could not find the institution of the papacy in Scripture. As for the Church Fathers, Luther argued that more could be cited against divine institution than for it.[4]

Hence Luther sought to demolish what he called the three walls papacy had built around itself: "the idea that the pope was not subject to any temporal authority, that only the pope could interpret Scripture, and that only the pope could call a general council of the church."[5]

3. It is interesting to note that in 1540, when he was challenged by more radical reformers, Luther admitted that there is much that is good and Christian in the papal church:

> We on our part confess that much is Christian and good under the papacy; indeed everything that is Christian and good is to be found there and has come from that source. For instance,... the true holy scriptures, true baptism, the true sacrament of the altar, the true keys to the forgiveness of sins, the true office of the ministry, the true catechism in the form of the Lord's prayer, the ten commandments, and the articles of the creed.[6]

If this is true why then did Luther criticize the Roman Church and regard the pope as antichrist? Luther's answer:

> Because [the pope] does not keep these treasures of Christendom which he has inherited from the apostles. He makes additions of the devil and does not use these treasures for the improvement of the temple. Instead, he works toward its destruction by setting his commandments above the ordinance of Christ. But Christ preserves his Christendom even in the midst of such destruction....In fact both remain: the antichrist sits in the temple of God (2 Thessalonians 2:3-4), while the temple still is and remains the temple of God through the power of Christ.[7]

4. Luther held that a general council of the church was a higher authority than the pope. This was a Conciliaristview which was widely held in Germany in 16th century. But Luther's acceptance of the council's authority was qualified. During his disputation with Johann Eck in Leipzik in 1519, Luther articulated his position thus:

> I agree with the lord doctor that the statutes of the councils in those things that concern the faith ought to be honored in every way. I reserve for myself this alone, which indeed must be reserved, that a council has erred at times and is able to err at any time, especially in those things that do not concern the faith. Nor does a council have authority to establish new articles of faith, otherwise we would have as many such articles as there are human opinions.[8]

How did Vatican II respond to this challenge of Luther? The Council's response can be summed up in three points.

1. "In virtue of his office, that is, as Vicar of Christ and pastor of the Church, the Roman Pontiff has full, supreme and universal power over the Church. And he can always exercise the power freely.[9] The Council adds: "For the Lord made Simon Peter alone the rock and key bearer of the Church (See Mt 16:18-19), and appointed him shepherd of the whole flock (See Jn 21:15 ff.).[10] "And all this teaching (of Vatican I) about the institution, the perpetuity, the force and reason for the sacred primacy of the Roman Pontiff… this sacred synod again proposes to be firmly believed by all this faithful.[11]

In this connection it is worth noting that a growing number of non-Catholic Christian theologians now accept the pope as a sign and unity of the Church.[12]

2. Vatican II has made two statements about the bishops which are important for the Council's understanding of Church authority.

a. The Council has taught that the college of bishops together with and under the pope is the subject of supreme power over the universal Church.[13]
Unfortunately Vatican II made no serious effort to reconcile its teaching on the collegiality of bishops with the dogma of the primacy of the pope defined by Vatican I and repeatedly cited by it. How many subjects of supreme authority are there in the Church?
Some believe that there are two – the pope alone and the college of bishops together with the pope. But I am inclined to agree with Karl Rahner when he states:

> It seems more correct and simpler to say that, juridically speaking, there is only one wielder of supreme power: the college constituted under the Pope as its primatial head. This does not exclude, but rather implies, that the Pope for his part can act "alone" as primate, since in such an action he need not make use of a regularly constituted collegial act in the strict sense. But even so, he always acts as head of the college, since this does not mean that he has to be lawfully delegated and appointed for such an act by the other bishops. We have already indicated that every primatial action of the Pope contains de facto a reference to the college as a whole."[14]

The Council seems to favour this view in its formulation of infallibility of the pope. While defining the pope's infallibility Vatican I made no reference to the college of bishops. But Vatican II teaches that the pope as head of the college enjoys infallibility.[15] What is said here of the teaching authority of the can be rightly be extended to all aspects of his authority.

b. The Council teaches that a person becomes a member of the college by the reception of a sacrament – the episcopate.[16] Like all sacraments the episcopate is of divine origin. This is of some importance for the understanding of the structure of the Church. Whatever be the mode of appointment of a bishop

– and today it is by a papal decision – the episcopate exists in the Church not through the kind favour of the pope. And the pope cannot choose to abolish it. The sacramentality of the episcopal ordination guarantees the continued existence of the episcopate as a constitutive element of the Church.

3. Vatican II has clearly spelt out the conditions under which the pope and the college of bishops together with the pope are infallible as well as the extent of their infallibility. The pope as head of the college enjoys infallibility "when, as the supreme shepherd and teacher of all the faithful, who confirms his brethren in their faith (See Lk 22:32), he proclaims by a definitive act some doctrine of faith or morals."[17] Something similar can be said of the infallibility of the college of bishops together with the pope.

The Council goes on to state that "this infallibility....extends as far as the deposit of divine revelation which must be religiously guarded and faithfully expounded."[18] Many theologians hold that the pope and the college of bishops are infallible when they teach some truths like the existence of God, the fact of revelation etc. which are not revealed, but which are necessary to guard and expound the deposit of revelation.

2. The Challenge of Scripture Alone

During the Imperial Dictof 1521 held at Worms, Luther was asked if he stood by all that he had written or if he wished to disown some of it. The representative of Emperor Charles V asked Luther for a clear and simple answer. This was Luther's reply:

> Since then your serene majesty and your lordships seek a simple answer, I will give it in this manner, neither horned nor toothed: Unless I am convinced by the testimony of Scriptures or by clear reason (for I do not trust either in the pope or in councils alone, since it is well known that they have often erred and contradicted themselves), I am bound by the Scriptures I have quoted and my conscience is captive to the Word of God. I cannot and I will not retract anything, since it is neither safe nor right to go against conscience. I cannot do otherwise, here I stand, may God help me. Amen.[19]

The touchstone of Luther's interpretation of the Scriptures was the Gospel, which he defined as "a discourse about Christ, that he is the son of God, and became human for us, that he died and was raised, that he has been established Lord over all things." In his preface to the New Testament, he placed the gospel of John and the epistles of Paul and Peter above the other books: "They showed Christ and taught everything that was necessary to know about salvation. Luther believed that "All genuine sacred books agree in this, that all of them preach and inculcate Christ.[20]

Scott H. Hendrix has pointed out that we need to have a nuanced understanding of Luther's view on Scripture alone:

> 'Scripture alone' *(sola scriptura),* which for some became the motto of the Protestantism, never meant for Luther that the Bible was the exclusive authority on every issue or that it offered a clear-cut, objective answer to every question. It did mean that on matters of dispute in the church it was the chief authority. The formula 'scripture alone' arose in Luther's conflict with the papacy as a statement of the Bible's superiority over the opinions of earlier theologians, the rules of canon law, and the decrees of councils and of popes.[21]

Now how does Vatican II respond to Luther's contention of "scripture alone"? The Council makes two statements.

1. It emphasizes the importance of Scripture in the life of the Church. In the Dogmatic Constitution on Divine Revelation the Council declares:

> The Church has always venerated the divine Scriptures just as she venerates the body of the Lord, since from the table of both the word of God and of the body of Christ she unceasingly receives and offers to the faithful the bread of life, especially in the sacred liturgy. She has always regarded the Scriptures together with sacred tradition as the supreme rule of faith, and will ever do so. For, inspired by God and committed once and for all to writing, they impart the word of God Himself without change, and make the voice of the Holy Spirit resound in the words of the prophets and apostles. Therefore, like the Christian religion itself, all the preaching of the Church must be nourished and ruled by sacred Scripture. For in the sacred books, the Father who is in heaven meets His children with great love and speaks with them; and the force and power in the word of God is so great that it remains the support and energy of the Church, the strength of faith for her sons, the food of the soul, the pure and perennial source of spiritual life.[22]

2. Vatican II highlights the importance of tradition. It uses the term tradition in two senses: a. What is handed on? b. How it is transmitted? (the process of handing on)[23]

Now what is handed on consists of all that the apostles had received from the lips of Christ, from living with him, from what he did, or what they had learned through the prompting of the Holy Spirit.[24] Commenting on this J. Ratzinger (the later Pope Benedict XVI) wrote:

> The point is certainly not to play off the theology of salvation history against word theology, but in place of a narrowly doctrinal conception

> of revelation, as had been expressed in the Tridentine word theology, to open up a comprehensive view of the real character of revelation, which precisely because it is concerned with the whole man is founded not only on the word that Christ preached, but in the whole of the living experience of his person, thus embracing what is said and what is unsaid, what the apostles in their turn are not able to express fully in words, but which is found in the whole reality of the Christian existence of which they speak, far transcending the framework of what has been explicitly formulated in words.[25]

The Council sums this up by stating: "Now what was handed on by the apostles comprises everything that serves to make the people of God live their lives in holiness and increase their faith."[26]

Because of the comprehensive nature of what is transmitted there are different ways of handing it on. Vatican II teaches that the apostles handed on what they had received by oral preaching, by example and by ordinances.[27] It also points out how the church in her teaching and worship perpetuates and hands on to all generations all that she herself is and all that she believes.[28] Hence we can say tradition is primarily not a question of words and propositions, but the entire life of the believing, praying and worshipping community.

Vatican II makes two more statements which have a bearing on Luther's position. 1) "Hence there is a close connection and communication between sacred tradition and sacred scripture. 2) It is not from sacred scripture alone that the Church draws its certainty about everything which has been revealed."[29] This last sentence need not cause any problem from an ecumenical point of view. As Protestant theologian H. Ott says: "Moreover it is surely also true for a Protestant who has forgotten the basis of the Reformation that we do not acquire certainty about God's revelation only from Scripture, but also through preaching and the inner testimony of the Holy Spirit".[30]

3. The Challenge of Justification and Salvation

For Luther both justification and salvation are God's gift. This is how Luther describes the insight that he got about justification:

> I began to understand that the righteousnessof God meant that those who were righteous lived by a gift of God, which is the passive righteousness by which God justifies us through faith, as it is written: 'They who through faith are righteous shall live' (Habakkuk 2:4). I felt I was altogether born again and had entered paradise through open gates.[31]

The faith in question was trust in God's promises that were fulfilled in Christ Jesus.

In December 1525 Luther finished the book, *The Bondage of the Will.* In it he asserted quite clearly his belief that human beings depended entirely on God's grace for salvation. As Paul W. Robinson briefly summarises Luther's position: "The human will was completely bound, as the title suggests, by sin and unable to make any move towards God. Salvation was accomplished, therefore, not by any human choice but by God's choice and by God's gift."[32]

Now how does Vatican II respond to Luther's ideas on justification and salvation? The Council does not say much about justification since the Council of Trent had dealt with it at length. The Dogmatic Constitution on the Church quotes Romans 4:25: Christ "who was handed over to death for our trespasses and was raised for our justification". And the Decree on Ecumenism states: "Nevertheless all those justified by faith through baptism are incorporated into Christ".[33]

With regard to human freedom and salvation Vatican II makes three significant statements; 1. Authentic freedom is an exceptional sign of the divine image in the human being.[34] We remember that the image of God was a key idea in the Pastoral Constitution on the Church in the Modern World. 2. Since human freedom has been damaged by sin, only by help of God's grace can a man and woman bring a relationship with God into full flower.[35] It is quite clear that the Council does not agree with Luther when he says that human freedom has been destroyed by sin. 3. God has willed that the human being be left in the hand of his or her counsel so that he or she can seek his creator spontaneously, and come freely to utter and blissful perfection through loyalty to Him.[36] For Vatican II salvationis both God's gift and human achievement.

4. The Challenge of the Sacraments

Scott H. Hendrix has given a brief summary of Luther's views on the sacraments:

> In a 1520 treatise entitled *The Babylonian Captivity of the Church,* Luther argued that the seven sacraments of the late medieval church should be reduced to three: baptism, the Lord's Supper, and penance, the last of which he called confession and absolution. According to his definition, sacraments had to be commanded in scripture and attached to both a spiritual promise and a material element that were clearly audible and visible when the sacrament was administered. For Luther, only baptism and the Lord's Supper unequivocally fulfilled these requirements. Water was applied in baptism, and bread and wine were consumed in the Lord's Supper, but no physical element was involved in confession and absolution. Soon penance was no longer considered a sacrament - especially because it did no more than renew the lifelong promise of forgiveness and salvation bestowed at baptism.[37]

There are three more points in Luther's position on the sacraments. 1. Luther retained public and private confession, but abolished the element of penance. He believed that absolution from sin, whether private or public, took complete effect immediately because free forgiveness was guaranteed through baptism. "The promise of forgiveness and salvation applied in baptism was valid forever and became the foundation of Christian life at whatever age a person was baptized. For that reason, Luther retained infant baptism and considered it the most important sacrament"[38]2. Luther believed in the real presence of Jesus Christ in the Eucharist. He took quite seriously Jesus' words during the Last Supper: "This is my body" This is my blood". 3. Luther denied that Holy Eucharist was a sacrifice. He rejected the medieval interpretation of the Last Supper as a repetition of the sacrifice Jesus offered on the cross for the sins of humankind. He was against abuses like the multiplication of Masses which that interpretation made possible. "As a holy offering made by the priest, the Mass was easily considered a miraculous good work that could earn merit for laity who either watched the mass being performed or who paid priests to say regular posthumous Masses for themselves and their loved ones."[39] It was also true that some people thought that the more masses they attended the more merit would accrue to them

How did Vatican II respond to Luther's view on the sacraments?

The Second Vatican Council did not deal with the sacraments at length. It did not give a clear definition of the sacrament. But from the way it spoke of the different sacraments one can deduce that the Council accepted Trent's understanding of the sacrament. For the Council of Trent a sacrament had three aspects: 1. Sign aspect: Sacrament is a visible sign of invisible grace. 2. Agent aspect: The sacrament confers the grace it signifies. 3. Presence: The sacrament makes present the grace which it signifies and confers. So the sacrament is a symbol which contains the grace which it signifies and brings about.[40]

Trent's understanding of the sacrament is quite different from that of Luther. For him only that rite is a sacrament to which God's promise of forgiveness is attached. But Trent believes that God's dealings with the believers in the sacrament should not be restricted to the offer of the forgiveness of sin. God can through the sacrament give us grace to grow in spiritual life and effectively fulfil our Christian mission. Moreover, Christian can cooperate with God's grace, given through the sacrament, by fulfilling the purpose for which it is given.

All this is involved in the description of the sacraments Vatican II gives in the Dogmatic Constitution on the Church:

Incorporated into the Church through baptism, the faithful are consecrated by the baptismal character to the exercise of the cult of the Christian religion. Reborn as children of God, they must confess before men the faith which they have received from God through the Church. Bound more intimately to the Church by the sacrament of confirmation, they are endowed by the Holy Spirit with special strength. Hence they are more strictly obliged to spread and defend the faith both by word and by deed as true witnesses of Christ.

> Taking part in the Eucharistic Sacrifice, which is the fount and apex, of the whole Christian life, they offer the divine Victim to God, and offer themselves along with It. Thus, both by the act of oblation and through holy Communion, all perform their proper part in this liturgical service, not indeed, all in the same way but each in that way which is appropriate to himself. Strengthened anew at the holy table by the Body of Christ, they manifest in a practical way that unity of God's People which is suitably signified and wondrously brought about by this most awesome sacrament.[41]

The Council deals with the truth that the Eucharist is a sacrifice. In the Constitution on the Sacred Liturgy it declares:

> At the Last Supper, on the night when He was betrayed, our Saviour instituted the Eucharistic Sacrifice of His Body and Blood. He did this in order to perpetuate the sacrifice of the Cross throughout the centuries until He should come again, and so to entrust to His beloved spouse, the Church, a memorial of His death and resurrection: a sacrament of love, a sign of unity, a bond of charity, a paschal banquet in which Christ is consumed, the mind is filled with grace, and a pledge of future glory is given to us.[42]

5. The Challenge to Marian Piety

Luther's views on Marian piety can be summed up in four points:

1. He was against rituals or titles used in Marian devotion that infringed on the unique role of Jesus in the redemption of the human race. Hence Mary was not a co-redeemer with Jesus.
2. The title "queen of heaven" was in a sense true, but "it did not make her a goddess who could grant gifts or render aid as some suppose when they pray and flee to her rather than God."
3. The ancient title "mother of God" was the greatest thing a believer could say of her.[43]
4. Luther suggested that those who wish to honour Mary must not isolate her,

> but set her in the presence of God and far beneath God, strip her of all honour and regard her 'low estate' (Luke 1:48), then marvel at the exceedingly abundant grace of God, who regards, embraces, and blesses so despised a mortal.... She does not want you to come to her, but through her to God.[44]

How does Vatican II respond to Luther's views on Marian Piety? There are four points in the Council's response which I wish to highlight.

1. Vatican II decided not to have a separate document on the Blessed Virgin Mary. Instead it has a chapter in the Dogmatic Constitution on the Church, titled: The Role of The Blessed Virgin Mary, Mother of God, in The Mystery of Christ and The Church. Commenting on this Evelyn Monteiro has stated:

Inserting it in *Lumen Gentium* would also provide a balanced understanding of the mystery of the Church as both redeemed and redeeming by emphasizing Mary's relationship to the Church and Christ. Relating Mary to Christ and the Church would strengthen the devotional life of the faithful regarding the essentials of faith in the incarnation and redemption and Mary's unique role in these mysteries of faith. Finally, it would have ecumenical importance - Mary's role as *Theotokos* or God-bearer would enhance dialogue with the Orthodox Churches of the East, and the Protestants would be receptive to a biblical portrait of Mary as the type of the Church (Jn 18:25; Acts 2:14)[45]

2. The Council clearly affirms the unique mediatorship of Jesus Christ. It quotes 1 Timothy 2:5-6 which says that there is one mediator between God and humankind, Christ Jesus. Then it goes on to add:

> The maternal duty of Mary towards human beings in no way obscures or diminishes this unique mediation of Christ, but rather shows its power. For all the saving influences of the Blessed Virgin on human beings originate, not from some inner necessity, but from the divine pleasure. They flow forth from the superabundance of the merits of Christ, rest on His meditation, depend entirely on it, and draw all their power from it. In no way do they impede the immediate union of the faithful with Christ. Rather they foster this union.[46]

3. Vatican II asks theologians and pastors that, while dealing with the dignity of the Mother of God, they should avoid all exaggerations:

> But this Synod earnestly exhorts theologians and preachers of the divine word that in treating of the unique dignity of the Mother of God, they carefully and equally avoid the falsity of exaggeration on the one hand, and the excess of narrow-mindedness on the other. Pursuing the study of sacred Scripture, the holy fathers, the doctors, and liturgies of the Church, and under the guidance of the Church's teaching authority, let them rightly explain the offices and privileges of the Blessed Virgin which are always related to Christ, the Source of all truth, sanctity, and piety.
>
> Let them painstakingly guard against any word or deed which could lead separated brethren or anyone else into error regarding the true doctrine of the Church.[47]

4. The Council explains to the faithful the nature of true devotion to the Blessed Virgin Mary:

> Let the faithful remember moreover that true devotion consists neither in fruitless and passing emotion, nor in a certain vain credulity. Rather, it proceeds from true faith, by which we are led to know the excellence of the Mother or God, and are moved to a filial love toward our mother and to the imitation of her virtues.[48]

By way of conclusion I would like to say that Martin Luther was a great Christian who was deeply devoted to Jesus Christ and passionately attached to his gospel. He was a genuinely religious person who prayed and asked people to pray. He was a hard-working man who wrote a lot. His collected works run into 55 volumes of about 350 pages each. In eleven weeks he translated the New Testament into German. He was also musically gifted. He translated or composed more than 35 hymns, of which the best known was *A Mighty Fortress is our God.* Luther had no intention of dividing the Church or founding a new Church.

All that he wanted was to recover the authentic Christianity which he thought had been lost.

Notes

1. P. W. Robinson, *Martin Luther: A Life Reformed*, Boston: Longman, 2010, p. 25.
2. See G. Alberigo, "The Christian Situation after Vatican II," in G. Alberigo and others (eds.), *The Reception of Vatican II*, Washington: The Catholic University of America Press, 1987, p. 13.
3. P. W. Robinson, *Martin Luther:A Life Reformed*, p. 31.
4. *Ibid.* p. 29.
5. *Ibid.* p. 40.
6. As quoted by S. H. Hendrix, *Martin Luther: A Very Short Introduction*, New York: Oxford University Press, 2010, p. 47.
7. *Ibid.* pp. 47-48
8. As quoted by P. W. Robinson, *Martin Luther:A Life Reformed*, p. 30.
9. Vatican II, Dogmatic Constitution on the Church, Rome, 1964, p. 22.
10. *Ibid.*
11. *Ibid.* p. 18.
12. See K. Rahner and H. Fries, *Unity of the Church: An Actual Possibility*, Philadelphia: Fortress Press, 1985, pp. 59-82.
13. Vatican II, Dogmatic Constitution on the Church, p. 22
14. K. Rahner, "Commentary on Chapter III of the Dogmatic Constitution on the Church" in H. Vorgrimler, *Commentary on the Documents of Vatican II*, Vol. I, New York: Herder and Herder, 1967, p. 203.
15. Vatican II, Dogmatic Constitution on the Church, p. 25.
16. *Ibid.* p.22.
17. *Ibid.* p. 25.
18. *Ibid.*
19. As quoted in P. W. Robinson, *Martin Luther: A Life Reformed*, p. 45.
20. S. H. Hendrix, *Martin Luther: A Very Short Introduction,* p. 42.

13

MISERICORDIAE VULTUS

Reflections on a Recent Papal Document

On April 11, 2015, Pope Francis issued a Bull titled *Misericordiae Vultus* in which he announced the Year of Mercy which would begin on December 8, 2015, and end on November 20, 2016.

I. In the 2nd article of the Bull, the Pope highlights the importance of Mercy in the Christian scheme of things:

> We need constantly to contemplate the mystery of mercy. It is a wellspring of joy, serenity, and peace. Our salvation depends on it. Mercy: the word reveals the very mystery of the Most Holy Trinity. Mercy: the ultimate and supreme act by which God comes to meet us. Mercy: the fundamental law that dwells in the heart of every person who looks sincerely into the eyes of his brothers and sisters on the path of life. Mercy: the bridge that connects God and man, opening our hearts to the hope of being loved forever despite our sinfulness.[1]

There are six significant ideas contained in this text. Mercy is the fount of joy, serenity and peace in human life. Our salvation is founded on it. Mercy reveals the mystery of the Triune God – a God of compassion and mercy. Mercy is the supreme act by which God comes to meet sinful human beings. Mercy is the right attitude of every human being who clearly perceives the pathetic situation of his brothers and sisters during the journey of life. Mercy is the bond between God and humans, opening our hearts to the hope of being loved forever though we, because of our sinfulness, are unworthy of it.

II. In this Bull Pope Francis primarily deals with God's mercy as revealed in and through Jesus of Nazareth. As a background to it, he discusses the mercy of God manifested in the Old Testament. The Pope also touches on the development of this theme in the Church. Then he clarifies the relationship between justice and mercy. Finally Pope Francis spells out some of the ways in which we humans can show mercy.

1. God's Mercy in the Old Testament

As the Pope points out: "Patient and merciful. These words often go together in the Old Testament to describe God's nature."[2] We shall now discuss some texts which speak of God's mercy.

1) In the Exodus the Lord revealed himself to Moses "as a God merciful and gracious, slow to anger, and abounding in steadfast love and faithfulness, keeping steadfast love for the thousandth generation, forgiving iniquity and transgression and sin" (Ex 34: 6-7).
   God manifests his mercy and graciousness by forgiving iniquity and transgression and sin.
2) God's mercy is concretely demonstrated in his many actions in the history of salvation where his goodness prevails over punishment and destruction. In a special way, the Psalms describe the wonder of his merciful action: "He forgives all your iniquity, he heals all your diseases, he redeems your life from the pit, he crowns you with steadfast love and mercy (Ps 103:3-4).

Another Psalm speaks of the concrete signs of God's mercy: "He executes justice for the oppressed; he gives food for the hungry. The Lord sets the prisoners free; the Lord opens the eyes of the blind. The Lord lifts up those who are bowed down; the Lord loves the righteous. The Lord watches over the strangers; he upholds the orphan and the widow, but the way of the wicked he brings to ruin (Ps 146: 7-9).

In this context Pope Francis makes a relevant observation: "In short, the mercy of God is not an abstract idea, but a concrete reality with which he reveals his love as that of a father or mother, moved to the very depths out of love for their child."[3]

Psalm 136 is highly significant as it repeats after each verse the refrain: "For his mercy endures forever". As the Pope points out:

> By virtue of mercy, all the events of the Old Testament are replete with profound salvific import. Mercy renders God's history with Israel a history of salvation. To repeat continually "for his mercy endures forever," as the Psalm does, seems to break through the dimensions of space and time, inserting everything into the eternal mystery of love.[4]

3) The prophets of the Old Testament bear witness to God's mercy. Prophet Micah exclaims:
   Who is a God like you, pardoning inequity and passing over the transgression of the remnant of your possession? He does not retain his anger forever,

> because he delights in showing clemency. He will again have compassion upon us: he will tread our inequities under foot. You will cast all our sins into the depths of the sea (Mic 7:18-19).

Prophet Jonah also speaks of a God of mercy

O Lord, is not this what I said while I was still in my own country? That is why I fled to Tarshish at the beginning; for I knew that you are a gracious God and merciful, slow to anger, and abounding in steadfast love and ready to relent from punishing (Jon 4:2).

These words of Jonah need some explanation. God called Jonah and asked him to "go at once to Nineveh, that great city, and cry out against it; for their wickedness has come up before me" (Jon 1:2) But he did not want to go to Nineveh. Instead Jonah decided to flee to Tarshish and got into a ship that was going there. God intervened and prevented his going there. And "the word of the Lord came to Jonah a second time saying: Get up, go to Nineveh… and proclaim the message that I tell you" (3:1) And Jonah went into the city and cried out: "Forty days more and Nineveh shall be overcome"(3:41).

And the people of Nineveh including the king believed God. They repented of their sins and took to fasting and prayer. "When God saw what they did, how they turned from their evil ways, God changed his mind about the calamity that he had said that he would bring upon them; and he did not do it" (3:10).

Jonah became quite angry and told God why he did not want to be God's prophet. Because "God is a gracious God and merciful, slow to anger, steadfast in love, and ready to relent from punishing", Jonah was sure that God would let him down. See what a beautiful idea of God Jonah had.

2. Jesus and God's Mercy

Pope Francis opens, the bull with a powerful statement: "Jesus Christ is the face of the Father's mercy."[4] He goes on to add: "Mercy has become living and visible in Jesus of Nazareth, reaching its culmination in him… Jesus of Nazareth, by his words, his actions, and his entire person reveals the mercy of God."[5]

1) To begin with his actions. As the Pope points out: "The signs he works, especially in favour of sinners, the poor, the marginalized, the sick and the suffering are all meant to teach mercy."[6] In the Gospels terms like love, kindness, compassion and tenderness can all mean mercy.

When Jesus saw the crowds of people who followed him, he became aware that they were tired and exhausted, lost and without a guide and he felt deep compassion for them (see Matt 9:36). And because of his compassionate love he healed the sick who were brought to him (see Matt 14:14). He had compassion for the crowd which followed him for three days and had nothing to eat. The multiplication of the loaves and feeding of the four thousand people was the result of this compassion (see Matt 15:33-38). According to the Pope "What moved Jesus in all of these situations was nothing other than mercy with which he read the hearts of those he encountered and responded to their the needs. When he came upon the widow of Nain taking her son out for burial, he felt great compassion for the immense suffering of this grieving mother, and he gave back her son by raising him from the dead" (see Lk 7:13-15). After freeing the demoniac in the country of the Gerasenes Jesus told him: "Go home to your friends, and tell them how much the Lord has done for you, and what mercy he has shown you" (Mk 5:19).

2) Jesus' teaching on the mercy of God is contained in his parables of mercy. Luke has collected three of them-the lost sheep, the lost coin and the lost son – in chapter 15 of his gospel (see Lk 15: 1-32). In these parables, "Jesus reveals the nature of God as that of a Father who never gives up until he has forgiven the wrong and overcome rejection with compassion and mercy."[7]

While discussing these parables Robert J Karris observes: "God's mercy, indeed, is as foolish as the shepherd who abandons 99 sheep to save one, as a woman who turns her house upside down to recover a paltry sum, and as a Jewish father who joyfully welcomes home his wastrel son who has become a gentile."[8]

Pope Francis remarks: "In these parables, God is always presented as full of joy, especially when he pardons."[9] The shepherd, when he finds the lost sheep, calls together his friends celebrates his joy. And Jesus says: "Just so, I tell you, there will be more joy in heaven over one sinner who repents than over ninety-nine righteous persons who need no repentance" (Lk 15:7). The woman who finds her lost coin also asks her friends and neighbours to rejoice with her because she has found her lost coin. And Jesus remarks: "Just so, I tell you, there is joy in the presence of the angels of God over one sinner who repents "(Lk 15:10). And when the prodigal son returns his father celebrates. He tells the elder son: "But we had to celebrate and rejoice, because this brother of yours was dead and has come to life; he was lost and has been found" (Lk 15:31).

In these parables two understandings of God are in conflict. The Pharisees believed in a God who loved the just and hated the wicked. And so they thought that Jesus, if he came from this God, would do the same. But Jesus did not do so. Hence their complaint: "This fellow welcomes sinners and eats with them" (Lk 15:2). But Jesus believed in a God who loves and forgives sinners. To reveal this merciful God he welcomes sinners and eats with them. His table – fellowship with publicans and prostitutes was "a parable in action" which contains the message that God loves and forgives sinners.

The elder son in the parable is a spokesman for the Pharisees. Listen to what he says to the father:

Listen! For all these years I have been working like a slave for you, and I have never disobeyed your command; yet you have never given me even a young goat so that I might celebrate with my friends.[10] But when this son of yours came back, who has devoured your property with prostitutes, you killed the fatted calf for him!' (Lk 18: 11-12).

Compare the words of the elder son with the prayer of the Pharisee in the temple:

God, I thank you that I am not like other people: thieves, rogues, adulterers, or even like this tax collector. I fast twice a week; I give a tenth of all my income.' (Lk 18: 11-12).

At the end, one wonders who really is the lost son. The younger son goes away and lives riotously. But then he returns to the father, receives his forgiving love, rejoices in it and celebrates it. The elder son, a true Pharisee, does not think that he needs to repent and receive God's forgiving love. And he does not feel any joy which he can celebrate. He is really the lost son.

3. The Church and God's Mercy

The Church is entrusted with the mission of announcing the mercy of God. As the Pope points out: "Her life is authentic and credible only when she becomes a convincing herald of mercy. She knows that her primary task, especially at a moment full of great hopes and signs of contradiction, is to introduce everyone to the great mystery of God's mercy by contemplating the face of Christ. The Church is called above all to be a credible witness to mercy, professing it and living it as the core of the revelation of Jesus Christ."[11]

There is, however, a tendency in the Church to focus exclusively on justice to the neglect of mercy. In this context Pope Francis refers to the Encyclical of Saint John Paul II *Dives in Misericordia.*

The late Pope remarks:

> The present-day mentality, more than that of people in the past, seems to be opposed to a God of mercy, and in fact tends to exclude from life and to remove from the human heart the very idea of mercy. The word and the concept of 'mercy' seems to cause uneasiness in man who, thanks to the enormous development of science and technology, never before known in history, has become the master of the earth and has subdued and dominated it.[12]

A one-sided understanding of God which has no room for mercy is widespread today.

John Paul II goes on to state:

> The Church lives an authentic life when she professes and proclaims mercy – the most stupendous attribute of the Creator and of the Redeemer – and when she brings people close to the sources of the Saviour's mercy, of which she is the trustee and dispenser."[13]

The great theologian of the Church Thomas Aquinas declares: "It is proper to God to exercise mercy, and he manifests his omnipotence particularly in this way."[12] Thus mercy is not a sign of God's weakness but a mark of his omnipotence. This idea is taken up in the liturgy of the Church. In one of the ancient prayers of the liturgy the Church prays: "O God, who reveal your power above all in your mercy and forgiveness…"[14]

4. Justice and Mercy

Towards the end of the Bull Pope Francis seeks to clarify the relationship between justice and mercy. He begins by pointing out that "These are not two contradictory realities, but two dimensions of a single reality that unfolds progressively until it culminates in the fullness of love."[15]

Justice is a basic concept in civil society which is meant to be governed by the rule of law. Justice is also understood as giving each one what is rightly due to him/her. The Bible often speaks of divine justice and God as a Judge. In these passages, justice means the faithful observance of the law and the behaviour of every good Israelite who lives in accordance with God's commandments Such an understanding of justice, the Pope points out, "has not infrequently led to legalism by distorting the original meaning of justice and obscuring its profound value". We can go beyond this legalistic approach if we "recall that in Sacred Scripture justice is essentially conceived as the faithful abandonment of oneself to God's will."[16]

Jesus underlines the importance of mercy over against the observance of the law. While he was dining with Matthew and other tax collectors and sinners the Pharisees raised an objection. In defence of his behaviour Jesus says: "I desire mercy not sacrifice. I have not come to call the righteous, but sinners" (Matt 9:13). Commenting on this statement of Jesus, Pope Francis observes:

> Faced with a vision of justice as the mere observance of the law that judges people simply by dividing them into two groups – the just and sinners – Jesus is bent on revealing the great gift of mercy that searches out sinners and offers them pardon and salvation. One can see why, on the basis of such a liberating vision of mercy as a source of new life, Jesus was rejected by the Pharisees and the other teachers of the law.[17]

The company Jesus keeps with those the law considers sinners shows the depth of his mercy. In fact, mercy is revealed as a fundamental dimension of his mission.

In this connection the Pope refers to the life's journey of St Paul. Prior to his conversion Paul pursued the justice of the law with great zeal (see Phil, 3:6). After his conversion Paul adopted a totally different vision. Now he writes to the Galatians: "We have believed in Christ Jesus, in order to be justified by faith in Christ, and not by the works of the law, because by the works of law shall no one be justified" (Gal 2:16).

Paul's understanding of justice has undergone a radical change. He now gives priority to faith, not justice. "Salvation comes not through the observance of the law, but through faith in Jesus Christ, who, in his death and resurrection, brings salvation together with a mercy that justifies. God's justice now becomes the liberating force for those oppressed by slavery to sin and its consequences. God's justice is his mercy" (see Ps, 51: 11-16).[18]

Pope Francis now recalls the experience of Prophet Hosea to help us to see the way in which mercy surpasses justice. The Prophet lived in an era which was quite dramatic. The kingdom was about to be destroyed. The people of Israel had not remained faithful to the covenant. They had strayed from the right path and gone away from God and the faith of their forefathers. It seemed quite logical to believe that God will reject them and even destroy them. The Prophet hints at the possibility of their being sent into exile: "They shall return to the land of Egypt and Assyria shall be their King, because they have refused to return to me" (Hos 11:5).

And yet, after this hint of just punishment, the Prophet radically changes his words and reveals the true face of God:

> How can I give you up, O Ephraim? How can I hand you over, O Israel? How can I make you like Ad'mah? How can I treat you like Ze-boi'im? My heart recoils within me; my compassion grows warm and tender. I will not execute my fierce anger; I will not again destroy Ephraim for I am God and no mortal, the Holy One in your midst, and I will not come in wrath (Hos 11: 8-9).

It would seem that St. Augustine is commenting on the words of the prophet when he says: "It is easier for God to hold back anger than mercy". And Pope Francis adds: "God's anger lasts but a moment, his mercy forever."[19]

If God were concerned only with justice he would cease to be God. He would be like human beings who merely ask that the law be respected. This does not mean that justice is not important. Anyone who makes a mistake must pay a price. "However, this is just the beginning of conversion, not its end, because one begins to feel the tenderness and mercy of God. God does not deny justice. He rather envelopes it and surpasses it with an even greater event in which we experience love as the foundation of justice."[20]

As the Pope sums it up:

God's justice is his mercy given to everyone as a grace that flows from the death and resurrection of Jesus Christ. Thus the Cross of Christ is God's judgement on all of us and on the whole world, because through it he offers us the certitude of love and new life.[21]

Our Response to the Experience of God's Mercy

Pope Francis has spelt out some of the ways in which the Church as a whole and individual Christians can exercise mercy. I shall deal with them separately.

1. Church's Exercise of Mercy

1) The Church has to follow Jesus Christ and behave in the way he behaved. As the Pope emphatically states:

   Jesus went out to everyone without exception and manifested to them God's mercy. So "it is absolutely essential for the Church and for the credibility of her message that she herself live and testify to mercy. Her language and her gestures must transmit mercy, so as to touch the hearts of all people and inspire them once more to find the road that leads to the Father."[22]

2) The Church should carry the burden of the failures and struggles of the Christian people today. The time has come for the Church take up the joyful call to mercy once more. It is time to return to the basics and to bear the weakness and struggles of our brothers and sisters. Mercy is the force that reawakens us to new life and instills in us the courage to look to the future with hope.[23]

3) All pastoral activity of the Church has to be imbued with the spirit of mercy. As Pope Francis points out:

   Mercy is the very foundation of the Church's life. All of her pastoral activity should be caught up in the tenderness she makes present to believers; nothing in her preaching and in her witness to the world can be lacking in mercy. The Church's very credibility is seen in how she shows merciful and compassionate love.[24]

4) It is the mission of the Church to make present in this world the mercy of the Father. According to the Pope: "Consequently, wherever the Church is present, the mercy of the Father must be evident. In our parishes, communities, associations and movements, in a word, wherever there are Christians, everyone should find an oasis of mercy."[25]

5) It is the Church's duty to live in solidarity with the suffering and marginalized people and try to heal their wounds. Overcoming cold indifference and monotonous routine the Church has to open her eyes and see the misery of the world and the wounds of our brothers and sisters who are denied their dignity. "May we reach out to them and support them so they can feel the warmth of our presence, our friendship, and our fraternity! May their cry become our own, and together may we break down the barriers of indifference that too often reign supreme and mask our hypocrisy and egoism!.[26]

6) In the Church the confessors are called to be channels of God's mercy. The Pope has made this powerful statement:

   I will never tire of insisting that confessors be authentic signs of the Father's mercy. We do not become good confessors automatically. We become good confessors when, above all, we allow ourselves to be penitents in search of his mercy. Let us never forget that to be confessors means to participate in the very mission of Jesus to be a concrete sign of the constancy of divine love that pardons and saves. We priests have received the gift of the Holy Spirit for the forgiveness of sins, and we are responsible for this. None of us wields power over this Sacrament; rather, we are faithful servants of God's mercy through it.[27] Confessors are advised to follow the example of the father of the prodigal son and welcome repentant sinners with joy. Confessors should also go out to the other son who is resentful and incapable of rejoicing and help him to understand and accept the boundless love of the father.

They are not to ask useless questions. In short, confessors are called to be a sign of the primacy of mercy always, everywhere, and in every situation, no matter what."[28]

7) The Pope believes that the Church is closely related to Judaism and Islam, "both of which consider mercy to be one of God's important attributes. Israel was the first to receive this revelation which continues in history as an inexhaustible richness meant to be shared with all humankind…Among the privileged names that Islam attributes to the Creator are "Merciful and Kind". This invocation is often on the lips of faithful Muslims…"[29]

Pope Francis recommends that the Church foster a deeper encounter and a more fervent dialogue with these religions and other religious traditions in order that we may know and understand one another better. This is the Pope's desire and prayer: "May it eliminate every form of close-mindness and disrespect, drive out every form of violence and discrimination."[30]

2. The individual Christian's Exercise of Mercy

The Pope has made several concrete suggestions on how we Christians are to show mercy. I shall now discuss some of them.

1) Forgiveness

Pope Francis refers to the Parable of the Unforgiving servant (Matt 18: 23-35) in order to underline the importance of the practice of forgiveness in our life.

> This parable contains a profound teaching for all of us. Jesus affirms that mercy is not only an action of the Father; it becomes a criterion for ascertaining who his true children are. In short, we are called to show mercy because mercy has first been shown to us. Pardoning offences becomes the clearest expression of merciful love, and for us Christians it is an imperative from which we cannot excuse ourselves.[30]

It is important to remember the context in which this parable in narrated. Peter asks the question: How often should I forgive (my brother who has offended me)? As many as seven times? Jesus answers: Not seven times, but I tell you seventy-seven times. Then he tells the parable of the unforgiving servant. The question of the King in the parable brings out its message. "Should you not have had mercy on your fellow slave, as I had mercy on you" (Matt 18:33).

St Paul has put it succinctly: "As the Lord has forgiven you, so you must also forgive (Col 3:13)."

1) Be merciful like the Father

This is based on Luke 6:36. In this text Jesus asks us: "Be merciful just as your Father is merciful". In order to grasp the full import of this text we must pay attention to two things:

(1) The context (see Lk 6:27-35). In this passage Jesus commands his followers: Love your enemies, do good to those who hate you, bless those who curse you, pray for those who abuse you" (16:27). Jesus goes on to point out that if you love only those who love you; if you do good only to those who do good you; and if you lend only to those from whom you hope to receive, you are not doing anything great. Even sinners do so (see 6:33-34). Now Jesus emphatically declares: "Love your enemies, do good and lend expecting nothing in return. Your reward will be great and you will be children of the Most High; for he is kind to the ungrateful and the wicked" (6:35). Then Jesus draws the conclusion: "Be merciful, just as Father is merciful:. (6:36). What Jesus emphasizes here is this: It is by showing unconditional love and mercy that we become children of our Father in heaven.

(2) The parallel passage which is Matt 5:43-48. There, too, Jesus asks his followers: "Love your enemies and pray for those who persecute you" (see 5:44): Then he adds: "so that you may be children of your Father in heaven; for he makes his sun rise on the evil and on the good, and sends his rain on the righteous and the unrighteous" (5:45). We disciples of Jesus must practise unconditional love towards the good and the evil, the righteous and the unrighteous as the Father does. Then the conclusion: "Be perfect as your heavenly Father is perfect." It would seem that the Father's perfection consists in his unconditional love and mercy to sinful humans. And we are to be like our Father by showing unconditional love and mercy to our enemies and those who persecute us.

Pope Francis is aware that this is not easy. Hence he points out:

In order to be capable of mercy, therefore, we must first of all dispose ourselves to listen to the Word of God. This means rediscovering the value of silence in order to meditate on the Word that comes to us. In this way, it will be possible to contemplate God's mercy and adopt it as our lifestyle.[31]

2) "Do not judge" (Lk 6:37)

In order grasp the full import of this text from Luke's gospel let us read the whole text:

"Do not judge, and you will not be judged; do not condemn, and you will not be condemned. Forgive, and you will be forgiven; give, and it will be given to you. A good measure, pressed down, shaken together, running over, will be put into your lap; for the measure you give will be the measure you get back." (Lk 6:37-38)

Notice two things in the text: (1) we are not asked: do not judge harshly, but do not judge, full stop; (2) we need to distinguish between judging a person and evaluating his/her external behaviour. If you are a parent, teacher or format or you have the right and duty to evaluate the behaviour of the child / student / formee. If the novice mistress were to say that the way a young novice dresses is not modest, she is only evaluating the external behaviour of the novice. But if she takes the next step and says (or thinks) that this young novice is a bad person, then she is judging her. We have always to keep this distinction in mind.

Commenting on this text of Luke (6: 37-38) Pope Francis says:

> Human beings, whenever they judge, look no farther than the surface, whereas the Father looks into the very depths of the soul. How much harm words do when they are motivated by feelings of jealousy and envy! To speak ill of others puts them in a bad light, undermines their reputation and leaves them prey to the whims of gossip. To refrain from judgement and condemnation means, in a positive sense, to know how to accept the good in every person and to spare him any suffering that might be caused by our partial judgment, our presumption to know everything about him. But this is still not sufficient to express mercy. Jesus asks us also to forgive and to give. To be instruments of mercy because it was we who first received mercy from God. To be generous with others, knowing that God showers his goodness upon us with immense generosity.[32]

3) Works of the Mercy

The Pope expresses his burning desire that the Christian people reflect on the *corporal and spiritual works of mercy*. Then he adds:

> It will be a way to reawaken our conscience, too often grown dull in the face of poverty. And let us enter more deeply into the heart of the Gospel where the poor have a special experience of God's mercy. Jesus introduces us to these works of mercy in his preaching so that we can know whether or not we are living as his disciples. Let us rediscover these corporal works of mercy: to feed the hungry, give drink to the thirsty, clothe the naked, welcome the stranger, heal the sick, visit the imprisoned, and bury the dead. And let us not forget the spiritual works of mercy: to counsel the doubtful, instruct the ignorant, admonish sinners, comfort the afflicted, forgive offences, bear patiently those who do us ill, and pray for the living and the dead.[33]

In this connection, Pope Francis recalls Mathew 25: 31-46, which describes the judgment of the nations. There are three points to be made here (1) While performing these corporals works of mercy one does not need to see Jesus in the hungry, thirsty and the other needy people. Neither those on the right of the Lord nor those on his left recognized Jesus in the poor and the needy whom they served or did not serve; (2) In each of these little ones: Christ himself is present.

"His flesh becomes visible in the flesh of the tortured, the crushed, the scourged, the malnourished, and the exiled… to be acknowledged, touched, and cared for by us. Let us not forget the words of Saint John of the Cross. "As we prepare to leave this life, we will be judged on the basis of love"[34] (3) Mathew 25: 31-46 will serve as the criterion by which the ultimate success or failure of our life will be judged. At the end of our life we will not be asked: How often have you prayed? Or how many times did not fast? But we will be asked whether or not we have fed the hungry and given drink to the thirsty, welcomed the stranger and clothed the naked, or spent time with the sick and those in prison.

It may well be that we need to pray and fast often in order to be able to do these things.

Notes

1. *Misericordiae Vultus* (*MV*) 62.
2. Ibid n. 6.
3. Ibid.
4. Ibid n. 7.
5. Ibid n.1.
6. Ibid n. 8.
7. Ibid n. 9.
8. J. R. Karris, "The Gospel According to Luke", in R.E. Brown and others (eds.), *The New Jerome Biblical Commentary*, Eaglewood Cliffs: Prentice Hall, Inc., 1990, p. 707
9. Ibid.
10. Ibid. n. 25.
11. Ibid. n. 11.
12. Ibid. n. 12.
13. St Thomas Aquinas, *Summa Theologiae*, II – II, q. 30.a. 4
14. XXVI Sunday in Ordinary Time.
15. *MV* n. 20
16. Ibid.
17. Ibid.
18. Ibid.
19. *Homilies on the P salms 76,* 11.
20. *MV* n. 21.
21. Ibid.
22. Ibid n. 12.
23. Ibid n. 10.
24. Ibid.
25. Ibid n. 12.
26. Ibid. n. 15.
27. Ibid n. 17.
28. Ibid.
29. Ibid. n. 23.
30. Ibid.
31. Ibid n. 9.
32. Ibid n. 13.
33. Ibid n. 14.
34. Ibid n. 15.

14

CARING FOR OUR COMMON HOME

The Study of the Encyclical on Ecology

In May 2015 Pope Francis issued the Encyclical Letter *Laudato Si'* (Praise be to you) on the care for our common home. In this paper I shall briefly summarize the Encyclical and then reflect on it.

In the Introduction the Pope refers to five people who have exerted a lot of influence on his thinking. At first he speaks of St Francis of Assisi from whose canticle the title of the Encyclical is derived. Saint Francis, says the Pope, "reminds us that our common home is like a sister with whom we share our life and a beautiful mother who opens her arms to embrace us".[1] Pope Francis believes that Saint Francis is an inspiring example "of care for the vulnerable and of an integral ecology lived out joyfully and authentically".[2] According to the Pope:

> He is the patron saint of all who study and work in the area of ecology, and he is also much loved by non-Christians. He was particularly concerned for God's creation and for the poor and outcast. He loved, and was deeply loved for his joy, his generous self-giving, his openheartedness. He was a mystic and a pilgrim who lived in simplicity and in wonderful harmony with God, with others, with nature and with himself. He shows us just how inseparable the bond is between concern for nature, justice for the poor, commitment to society, and interior peace.[3]

Then comes Pope Paul VI who in 1971 declared: "Due to an ill-considered exploitation of nature, humanity runs the risk of destroying it and becoming in turn a victim of this degradation". He stressed "the urgent need for a radical change in the conduct of humanity", in as much as "the most extraordinary scientific advances, the most amazing technical abilities, the most astonishing economic growth, unless they are accompanied by authentic social and moral progress, will definitely turn against man".[4]

Pope John Paul II was deeply concerned about the ecological crisis. As a result, he called for an ecological *conversion*. He also pointed out that every effort to protect and improve our world entails profound changes in "lifestyles, models of production and consumption, and the established structures of power which today govern societies"[5].

Further, Pope Benedict XVI asked for "eliminating the structural causes of the dys functioning of the world economy and correcting models of growth which have proved incapable of ensuring respect for the environment". He pointed out that the world cannot be analyzed by one or other of its aspects since "the book of nature is one and indivisible". He was of the opinion that "the deterioration of nature is closely connected to the culture which shapes human coexistence". Creation is harmed when we human beings believe that we are its absolute masters: "The misuse of creation begins when we no longer recognize any higher instance than ourselves, when we see nothing else but ourselves".[6]

Pope Francis is very appreciative of the stand taken by the Ecumenical Patriarch Bartholomew. The Patriarch asks each of us to repent of our sins in causing damage to ecology, be it small or big. In his own words:

> For human beings... to destroy the biological diversity of God's creation; for human beings to degrade the integrity of the earth by causing changes in its climate, by stripping the earth of its natural forests or destroying its wetlands; for human beings to contaminate the earth's waters, its land, its air and its life – these are sins".[17]

Patriarch Bartholomew believes that the world is a sacrament of communion, a way of sharing with God and our neighbour on a global scale. "It is our humble conviction that the divine and the human meet in the slightest detail in the seamless garment of God's creation, in the last speck of dust of our planet".[8]

It is in this context that Pope Francis appeals to all humankind to seek together a sustainable and integral development:

> I urgently appeal, then, for a new dialogue about how we are shaping the future of our planet. We need a conversation which includes everyone, since the environmental challenge we are undergoing, and its human roots, concern and affect us all... We require a new and universal solidarity.[9]

Basing myself on Pope Francis' Encyclical I shall first describe some of the manifestations of the ecological crisis we are facing now. I shall then search for the causes of this crisis, that is, the human roots of this crisis. After that I shall develop some theological perspectives on this crisis. Then I shall project the vision of an integral ecology and spell out lines of approach and action in order to deal with this crisis. For the success of these efforts we need to impart to people an ecological education and develop a spirituality that will sustain us in dealing with this crisis effectively. By way of conclusion I shall reflect on the Encyclical and make some evaluative comments.

I. Main Insights of Pope Francis

1. Chapter one takes a critical look at what is happening to our common home. As the Pope makes it clear: "Our goal is not to amass information or to satisfy curiosity, but rather to become painfully aware, to dare to turn what is happening to the world into our own personal suffering and thus to discover what each of us can do about it."[10]

1.1 It is quite obvious that pollution in some form is part of people's daily experience. Exposure to pollutants in the atmosphere harms people's health and leads to millions premature deaths. As Pope Francis points out: People fall ill from breathing high levels of smoke from fuels used in cooking or heating. Everyone is affected by pollution caused by transport, industrial fumes, substances which pave the way for the acidification of air and water, fertilizers, insecticides, fungicides, herbicides and agrotoxins in general. In a way some of these evils are the result of a throwaway culture we have developed. We have not acquired, in a big way, the habit of recycling and reusing waste and the by-products of our industry. [11]

1.2 Climate change is a serious problem for all of us. According to Pope Francis:

> A very solid scientific consensus indicates that we are presently witnessing a disturbing warming of the climatic system. In recent decades this warming has been accompanied by a constant rise in the sea level and, it would appear, by an increase of extreme weather events, even if a scientifically determinable cause cannot be assigned to each particular phenomenon. Humanity is called to recognize the need for a change of lifestyle, production and consumption, in order to combat this warning or at least the human causes which produce or aggravate it.[12]

Global warming has serious consequences especially for the poor. It can cause a rise in the sea level which tends to create extremely serious situations, if we consider that a quarter of the world's population lives on the coast or nearby, and that the majority of our megacities are situated in coastal areas.[13]

It is important for us to realize that the poor are more seriously affected by climate change. They live in areas easily affected by climate change. Their means of subsistence, such as agriculture, fishing and forestry, is dependent on natural reserves. They have no alternative ways of earning a livelihood.[14]

1.3 The Issue of water, According to Pope Francis:

> Fresh drinking water is an issue of primary importance, since it is absolutely necessary for human life and for maintaining terrestrial and aquatic ecosystems. Availability of sufficient amount of water is indispensable for health care, agriculture and industry.[15]

In this connection one has to become aware of the poor quality of water available to the poor. But as Pope Francis declares:

> *Yet access to safe drinkable water is a basic and universal human right, since it is essential to human survival and, as such, is a condition for the exercise of other human rights.* Our world has a grave social debt towards the poor who lack access to drinking water, because they are denied the right to a life consistent with their inalienable dignity.[16]

1.4 The Loss of Biodiversity

The loss of biodiversity is a serious ecological problem. This is caused by short-sighted approaches to economy, commerce and production. The loss of many species of animals and plants causes untold harm. Many of them constitute "important resources for the future, not only for food but also for curing disease and other uses". These species are not only resources for the future, but they have a value in themselves.[17]

In this connection Pope Francis makes a pertinent observation:

It may well disturb us to learn of the extinction of mammals or birds, since they are more visible. But the good functioning of ecosystems also requires fungi, algae, worms, insects, reptiles and an innumerable variety of microorganisms. Some less numerous species, although generally unseen, nonetheless play a critical role in maintaining the equilibrium of a particular place.[8]

The Pope also refers to the harm done to the Amazon and Congo basins, to Virgin forests elsewhere and to the coral reefs in the ocean which shelter millions of species.

1.5 Decline in the Quality of Human Life

We need to consider the effects on people's lives of environmental deterioration, current models of development and the throwaway culture. We have become aware of the "unruly growth of many cities which have become unhealthy to live in" for a variety of reasons. Besides, "the social dimensions of global change include the effects of technological innovations on employment, social exclusion, an inequitable distribution and consumption of energy and other services, social breakdown, increased violence and a rise in new forms of aggression…"[19]

Pope Francis calls attention to the fact that the human environment and the natural environment are interdependent. They deteriorate together. We cannot adequately combat environmental degradation unless we attend to causes related to human and social degradation. In fact, the deterioration of the environment and of society affects the most vulnerable people on the planet."[20]

It is a sad truth that the poor and the marginalized and their problems are not prominent in the awareness of the international community. They are sometimes mentioned in political and economic discussions as an afterthought. "This is due partly to the fact that many professionals, opinion makers, communications media and centres of power, being located in affluent urban areas, are far removed from the poor, with little direct contact with their problems... Today, however, we have to realize that a true ecological approach always becomes a social approach; it must integrate questions of justice in debates on the environment, so as to hear *both the cry of the earth and the cry of the poor*".[21]

Pope Francis quotes with approval the words of the United States bishops: Greater attention must be given to "the needs of the poor, the weak and the vulnerable, in a debate often dominated by more powerful interests". We need to strengthen the conviction that we are one single human family. There are no frontiers or barriers, political or social, behind which we can hide, still less is there room for the globalization of indifference.[22]

Pope Francis concludes the chapter with the memorable words of Pope John Paul II: "If we scan the regions of our planet, we immediately see that humanity has disappointed God's expectations."[23]

II. Human Roots of the Ecological Crisis

Pope Francis is quite convinced that human beings and their activity are the root cause of the ecological crisis we are facing today: "A certain way of understanding human life and activity has gone awry, to the serious detriment of the world around us".[24] A mindless application of our technological power has caused enormous harm to the environment.

The Pope readily admits that the development of science and technology has been greatly beneficial to humankind. He acknowledges that technoscience can help to improve the quality of human life. It has produced a variety of things that can enhance human life – "from useful domestic appliances to great transportation systems, bridges, buildings, and public spaces". It can also produce art and enable people to leap into the world of beauty. "Valuable works of art and music now make use of new technologies. So, in the beauty intended by the one who uses new technical instruments and in the contemplation of such beauty, a quantum leap occurs, resulting in a fulfilment which is uniquely human".[25]

Technological progress has given tremendous power to human beings. Not to all of them but to those with knowledge and economic resources to use them. There is a tendency in many people to believe that every increase in power marks real human progress. The fact is that most people are not trained to use power wisely and well. Our immense technological development has not been accompanied by comparable ethical growth – "in human responsibilities, values and conscience". Here the Pope reminds us:

> But human beings are not completely autonomous. Our freedom fades when it is handed over to the blind forces of the unconscious, of immediate needs, of self-interest, and of violence. In this sense, we stand naked and exposed in the face of our ever-increasing power, lacking the wherewithal to control it. We have certain superficial mechanisms, but we cannot claim to have a sound ethics, a culture and spirituality genuinely capable of setting limits and teaching clear-minded self-restraint.[26]

Pope Francis believes that the globalization of the technocratic paradigm is at the root of the ecological crisis we are facing today.

Many of the problems in today's world stem from the tendency "to make the method and aims of science and technology an epistemological paradigm which shapes the lives of individuals and the workings of society". The deterioration of the environment is a clear sign of the bad effects of imposing this model on reality, human and social. This is, however, just one sign of the reductionism which affects every aspect of human and social life. "We have to accept that technological products are not neutral, for they create a framework which ends up conditioning lifestyles and shaping social possibilities along the lines dictated by the interests of certain powerful groups. Decisions which may seem purely instrumental are in reality decisions about the kind of society we want to build".[27]

The technological paradigm has become so dominant that it would be difficult to imagine life independent of it. "It has become counter- cultural to choose a lifestyle whose goals are even partly independent of technology, of its costs and its power to globalize and make us all the same." Technology tends to absorb everything into its ironclad logic, and those who are surrounded with technology "know full well that it moves forward in the final analysis neither for profit nor for the well-being of the human race", that "in the most radical sense of the term power is its motive-a lordship over all". As a result, "man seizes hold of the naked elements of both nature and human nature". Our capacity to make decisions, a more genuine freedom and the space for each one's alternative creativity are diminished.[28]

The technocratic paradigm exerts a lot of influence on economic and political life. The economy accepts every advance in technology because of profit. It is sad that we have not assimilated the lessons of the global financial crisis. And we appear to be quite slow in learning the lessons of environmental degradation.

Specialization which belongs to science and technology leads to a fragmentation of knowledge. And this prevents us from seeing the larger picture. This in turn leads to "a loss of appreciation for the whole, for the relationship between things, and for the broader horizon which then becomes irrelevant".

This very fact makes it hard to find adequate ways of solving the more complex problems of today's world, particularly those regarding the environment and the poor, these problems cannot be dealt with from a simple perspective or from a single set of interests. Anyone who wants to find solutions to the great problems of our time needs to take into consideration more than what can science can offer. He has to take into account data generated in other fields of knowledge, including philosophy and ethics. Humanity has not developed a genuine ethical horizon which can help us here.[29]

We need to realize that we have the freedom to limit and redirect technology. We are able to put it at the service of another kind of progress, "one which is healthier, more human, more social, more integral". We can adopt less polluting means of production and opt more for a non-consumerist model of life, recreation and community. Technology can be directed primarily to resolving people's concrete problems, truly helping them to live with more dignity and less suffering.[30]

Humanity urgently needs to move forward "in a bold cultural revolution". "We need to slow down and look at reality in a different way, to appropriate the positive and sustainable progress which has been made, but also to recover the values and the great goal, swept away by our unrestrained delusions of grandeur".[31]

Critique of Modern Anthropocentrism

Modern Anthropocentrism has several dimensions. Human beings are often tempted to place themselves at the centre of the whole universe. This leads to disastrous consequences.

1) Often an inadequate presentation of Christian Anthropology has led to a wrong understanding of the relationship between human beings and the environment. Often, what was handed on was a promethean vision of mastery over the world which gave the impression that protection of nature was something that only the faint-heated care about".[32]
2) Technology which sees no intrinsic value in lesser beings is in conflict with the other opinion that human beings have no special value. "But one cannot prescind from humanity. There can be no renewal of our relationship with nature without a renewal of humanity itself. There can be no ecology without an adequate anthropology".[33]
3) Modern anthropocentrism has been deeply affected by the technological mind which "sees nature as a insensate order, as a cold body of facts, as a mere given, even as an object of utility, as raw material to be hammered into useful shape; it views the cosmos similarly as mere 'space' into which objects can be thrown with complete indifference" The intrinsic dignity of the world is denied. When human beings are not conscious of their real place in the world they tend to go against themselves. They show no real respect for the nature of things nor for their own nature

as created beings. Human beings are called to respect the natural and moral structure with which they have been endowed.[34]

4) A misguided anthropocentrism leads to a misguided lifestyle. When human beings place themselves at the centre, they give priority to immediate convenience and all else becomes relatively insignificant. In this context Pope Francis pleads for the protection of employment. "In order to continue providing employment, it is imperative to promote an economy which favours productive diversity and business creativity. Economies of scale, especially in the agricultural sector, end up forcing small holders to sell their land or to abandon traditional crops".[35]

III. Theological Perspectives

Right at the beginning of chapter two the Pope asks a question: Why should this document, addressed to all people of good will, include a chapter dealing with the conviction of believers? And his answer: "Given the complexity of the ecological crisis and its multiple causes, we need to realize that the solutions will not emerge from just one way of interpreting and transforming reality. Respect must also be shown for the various cultural riches of different peoples, their art and poetry, their interior life and spirituality".[36] In this connection the Pope advocates an intense dialogue between science and religion which will be fruitful for both.[37]

Pope Francis also wishes to show Christians and other believers how faith convictions offer ample motivation to care for nature and for the most vulnerable of their brothers and sisters. Christians ought to "realize that their responsibility within creation, and their duty towards nature and the Creator, are an essential part of their faith". And it is good for humanity and the world at large if we believers clearly acknowledge the ecological commitments which stem from our faith convictions".[38]

1. The dignity of the human person

In the Book of Genesis, after the creation of man and woman, "God saw everything that he has made, and behold it was very good" (Gen 1:31). Every man and woman is created in the image and likeness of God (Gen 1: 26). Reflecting on this Pope Francis states: This shows us the immense dignity of each person, "who is not just something, but someone. He is capable of self-knowledge, of self-possession and of freely giving himself and entering into ommunion with other persons".[39] Saint John Paul II stated that the special love of the Creator for each human being "confers upon him or her an infinite dignity". Those who are committed to defending human dignity can find in the Christian faith the deepest reasons for this commitment. How wonderful is the certainty that each human life is not adrift in the midst of hopeless chaos, in a world ruled by pure chance or endlessly recurring cycles! The Creator can say to each one of us: "Before I formed you in the womb, I knew you" (Jer 1:5). We were conceived in the heart of God, and for this reason "each of us is the result of a thought of God. Each of us is willed, each of us is loved, each of us is necessary".[40]

2. Three fundamental relationships:

The creation accounts in Genesis suggest that human life is grounded in three fundamental and closely intertwined relationships: with God, with our neighbour and with the earth itself. As Genesis points out these three vital relations have been broken, both outwardly and within us. "The harmony between the Creator, humanity and creation as a whole was disrupted by our presuming to take the place of God and refusing to acknowledge our creaturely limitations. … As a result, the originally harmonious relationship between human beings and nature became conflictual" (Gen 3:17-19).[41]

3. Human beings have no absolute dominion over other creatures.

It is often said that the Judaeo-Christian thinking, based on the Genesis account which grants human beings "dominion" over the earth, has encouraged the unbridled exploitation of nature. As the Pope observes:

> This is not a correct interpretation of the Bible as understood by the Church. Although it is true that we Christians have at times incorrectly interpreted the Scriptures, nowadays we must forcefully reject the notion that our being created in God's image and given dominion over the earth justifies absolute domination over other creatures. The biblical texts are to be read in their context, with an appropriate hermeneutic, recognizing that they tell us to "till and keep" the garden of the world (cf. Gen 2:15). "Tilling" refers to cultivating, ploughing or working, while "keeping" means caring, protecting, overseeing and preserving. This implies a relationship of mutual responsibility between human beings and nature. "The earth is the Lords" (Ps 24:1); to him belongs "the earth with all that is within it" (Dt 10:14). Thus God rejects every claim to absolute ownership: "The land shall not be sold in perpetuity, for the land is mine; for you are strangers and sojourners with me" (Lev 25:23).[42]

4. The Bible rejects tyrannical anthropocentrism.

It is part of humans' responsibility for God's earth that they respect the laws of nature and the delicate equilbria existing between the creatures of the world, for "he commanded and they were created, and he established them for ever and ever; he fixed their bounds and he set a law which cannot pass away (Ps 148:5b-6). "The laws found in the Bible dwell on relationships, not only among individuals but also other living beings. Thus the rest on the Sabbath day is not meant only for human beings but also for other creatures so "that your ox and your donkey may have rest" (Ex 23:12).[43]

These days the Church does not simply state that all other creatures are completely subordinated to the welfare of human beings as though they have no value in themselves. The German Bishops have said that when other creatures are concerned "we can speak of the priority of *being* over than of *being useful*". And the Catechism of the Catholic Church clearly teaches: "Each creature possesses its own particular goodness and perfection... Each of the various creatures, willed in its own being, reflects in its own way a ray of God's infinite wisdom and goodness. Man must therefore respect the particular goodness of every creature, to avoid any disordered use of things".[44]

To sum up: Pope Francis is quite convinced that "the Bible has no place for tyrannical anthropocentrism unconcerned for other creatures".

Care for the earth and concern for our brothers are interconnected. Referring to the biblical story of Cain and Abel (Genesis chapter 4) and the story of Noah (Genesis 6-7) the Pope observes: "These ancient stories, full of symbolism, bear witness to a conviction which we today share, that everything is interconnected, and that genuine care for our own lives and our relationships with nature is inseparable from fraternity, justice and faithfulness to others.[45]

1. Acknowledging God as the all-powerful Creator is liberating. According to Pope Francis: A spirituality which forgets God as all-powerful Creator is not acceptable. That is how we end up worshipping earthly powers, or ourselves usurping the place of God, even to the point of claiming an unlimited right to trample his creation under foot.[46]
2. Creation is the gift of God's love:
   "By the word of the Lord the heavens were made" (Ps 33:6
   Creation is of the order of love. God's love is the fundamental moving force in all created things: "For you love all things that exist, and detest none of the things that you have made; for you would not have made anything if you had hated it" (Wis 11:24). Every creature is thus the object of the Father's tenderness, who gives it its place in the world. Even the fleeting life of the least of beings is the object of his love, and in its few seconds of existence, God enfolds it with his affection.[47]
3. Judaeo-Christian thought demythologized nature. While it admires the grandeur and the immensity of the world, it does not consider it to be divine. "In doing so, it emphasizes all the more our responsibility for nature". As part of the world, human beings, endowed with freedom and responsibility, have the duty to cultivate their abilities to protect the world and develop its potential".[48]
   If we acknowledge the value and the fragility of nature and, at the same time, our God-given abilities, we can finally leave behind the modern myth of unlimited material progress. A fragile world, entrusted by God to human care, challenges us to devise intelligent ways of directing, developing and limiting our power.

4. The Uniqueness of human beings:

In the Christian scheme of things human beings are unique. As Pope Francis clarifies:" Each of us has his or her own personal identity and is capable of entering into dialogue with others and with God himself. Our capacity to reason, to develop arguments, to be inventive, to interpret reality and to create art, along with other not yet discovered capacities, are signs of a uniqueness which transcends the spheres of physics and biology".[56] The biblical accounts of creation invite us to see each human being as a subject who can never be reduced to the status of an object.[49]

5. Every creature has a message for us from God. God has written a precious book, "whose letters are the multitude of created things present in the universe". The Canadian bishops rightly pointed out that no creature is excluded from this manifestation of God: "From panoramic vistas to the tiniest living form, nature is a constant source of wonder and awe. It is also a continuing revelation of the divine". The bishops of Japan, for their part, made a thought-provoking observation: "To sense each creature singing the hymn of its existence is to live joyfully in God's love and hope". This contemplation of creation allows us to discover in each thing a teaching which God wishes to hand on to us, since "for the believer, to contemplate creation is to hear a message, to listen to a paradoxical and silent voice". We can say that "alongside revelation properly so-called, contained in Sacred Scripture, there is a divine manifestation in the blaze of the sun and the fall of night".[50]

Saint Thomas Aquinas explains the multiplicity and variety of creatures in the world thus. "What was wanting to one in the representation of the divine goodness might be supplied by another". It is clear that God's goodness cannot be fittingly represented by any one creature. Hence we need to understand the variety of creatures in their manifold relationships. As the Catechism of the Catholic Church teaches: "God wills the interdependence of creatures in the service of each other".[51]

All created things belong to the Lord who loves them. As Pope Francis observes: "This is the basis of our conviction that, as part of the universe, called into being by one Father, all of us are linked by unseen bonds and together form a kind of universal family, a sublime communion which fills us with a sacred, affectionate and humble respect".[59]Besides "God has joined us so closely to the world around us that we can feel the desertification of the soil almost as a physical ailment, and the extinction of a species as a painful disfigurement".[52]

We should never forget that "Peace, justice and the preservation of creation are three absolutely interconnected themes, which cannot be separated and treated individually without once again falling into reductionism".[53] Everything is related, and we human beings are united as brothers and sisters on a wonderful pilgrimage, woven together by the love God has for each of his creatures and which also unites us in fond affection with brother sun, sister moon, brother river and mother earth.

6. The Universal Destination of All Goods.

Christian tradition has always maintained that God created the world for everyone. Hence "the earth is essentially a shared inheritance, whose fruits are meant to benefit everyone". It is important to remember that the Christian tradition "has never recognized the right to private property as absolute or inviolable and has stressed the social purpose of all forms of private property".[54]

In this connection Pope Francis quotes New Zealand bishops who ask: "What the commandment "Thou shall not kill" means when "twenty percent of the world's population consumes resources at a rate that robs the poor nations and future generations of what they need to survive".[55]

Jesus told us that each one of the creatures is important in God's eyes.

Jesus emphasized the fundamental truth that God is Father and has a paternal relationship with all his creatures. "Are not five sparrows sold for two pennies? And not one of them is forgotten before God" (Lk 12:6). Again, "Look at the birds of the air; they neither sow nor reap nor gather into barns, and yet your heavenly Father feeds them" (Matt 6:26). As he wandered throughout the land Jesus often stopped to contemplate beauty sown by his Father. And he asked the disciples to discover the divine message in things: "Lift up your eyes, and see how the fields are already white for harvest" (Jn 4:35).

Jesus was certainly not an ascetic who was the enemy of the pleasant things of life. "The Son of Man came eating and drinking and they say: Look, a glutton and a drunkard" (Matt 11:19). He did not subscribe to the philosophies which despised the body, matter and the things of the world.[56]

IV. Integral Ecology

In Chapter Four Pope Francis discusses five elements of an integral ecology, one which clearly respects its human and social dimensions

1. Environmental, economic and social ecology. The Pope begins by pointing out danger of the fragmentation of knowledge: "It cannot be emphasized enough how everything is interconnected. It follows that the fragmentation of knowledge and the isolation of bits of information can actually become a form of ignorance, unless they are integrated into a boarder vision of reality".[57]

When we a speak of the environment what we mean is this: The relationship that exists between nature and the society which lives in it. Nature is not completely separate from ourselves. We are part of nature and are in continual interaction with it.[58]

There is need for an "economic ecology" which is capable of appealing to a broader vision of reality. We have to realize that the protection of the environment is "an integral part of the development process and cannot be considered in isolation from it". We need a humanism capable of bringing together the different fields of knowledge, including economics, in the service of a more integral and integrating vision. "Today, the analysis of environmental problems cannot be separated from the analysis of human, family, work related and urban contexts, nor from how individuals relate to themselves, which leads in turn to how they relate to others and to the environment".[59]

It is important to realize that the good health of a society's institutions has consequences for the environment and the quality of human life. "Every violation of solidarity and civic friendship harms the environment". Social ecology is necessarily institutional. Anything that weakens the institutions of society has negative consequences, such as injustice, violence and loss of freedom. It is not enough to frame good laws. They must be strictly enforced. Only then these laws can protect the environment.[60]

2. Cultural ecology. It is not only nature that is under threat. The historic, artistic and cultural patrimony of people is under threat. As Pope Francis points out: "Rather, there is a need to incorporate the history, culture and architecture of each place, thus preserving its original identity. Ecology, then, also involves protecting the cultural treasures of humanity in the broadest sense. More specifically, it calls for greater attention to local cultures when studying environmental problems, favouring a dialogue between scientific-technical language and the language of the people". Culture is not just an inheritance from the past but also a dynamic and participatory present reality, which cannot be excluded as we rethink the relationship between human beings and the environment.[61]

While taking steps to protect nature the culture of the local people must be taken into account. As the Pope observes: Merely technical solutions run the risk of addressing symptoms and not the more serious underlying problems. There is a need to respect the rights of peoples and cultures, and to appreciate that the development of a social group presupposes an historical process which takes place within a cultural context and demands the constant and active involvement of local people from within their proper culture.[62] The idea of the quality of life cannot be imposed from without, for quality of life must be understood within the world of symbols and customs proper to each human group.

Pope Francis remarks that "the disappearance of a culture can be just as serious, or even more serious, than the disappearance of a species of plant or animal".[63] Hence one has to be careful not to impose a dominant lifestyle linked to a single form of production. It can be just as harmful as altering ecosystems.

Pope Francis points out that the setting of our life can affect the quality of our life: "Authentic development includes efforts to bring about an integral improvement in the quality of human life, and this entails considering the setting in which people live their lives. These settings influence the way we think, feel and act".[64]

It is obvious that urban planning should take seriously the views of those who will live in those areas. This is so because there is an interrelationship between living space and human behaviour.

Lack of housing is a grave problem both in the cities and rural areas. Many members of society, besides the poor, find it difficult to own a home. "Having a home has much to do with a sense of personal dignity and the growth of families". Warm human relationships can do a lot to make rundown neighbourhoods happy. As the Pope points out: "How beautiful those cities which overcome paralyzing mistrust, integrate those who are different and make this very integration a new factor of development! How attractive are those cities which, even in their architectural design, are full of spaces which connect, relate and favour the recognition of others".[65]

Systems of transport in our big cities are a serious problem causing much suffering to those who use them. The large number of cars, used by one or two people, circulate in our cities, causing traffic jam, raising the level of pollution and consuming enormous quantities of non-renewal energy. We need to give priority to public transport, but to be really useful it must be improved substantially.[66]

3. The Principle of Common Good

Pope Francis believes that the notion of the common good is a central and unifying principle of social ethics. To explain this notion he quotes Vatican II: The common good is "the sum of those conditions of social life which allows social groups and their individual members relatively thorough and ready access to their own fulfilment".[67]

The principle of the common good is derived from three basic elements:

1) Respect for the human person who is endowed with fundamental inalienable rights ordered to his/her integral development
2) The overall welfare of society and the development of intermediate groups. Foremost among these groups is the family, the basic cell of society
3) Concern for social peace, the stability and security provided by a certain order which cannot be achieved without genuine commitment to distributive justice. Whenever this is violated, violence always ensues. The Pope is convinced that "Society as a whole, and the state in particular, is obliged to defend and promote the common good:"[68]

At present injustices abound in global society and a large number of people are deprived of their basic human reights. Here "the principle of the common good immediately becomes, logically and inevitably, a summons to solidarity and a preferential option for the poorest of our brothers and sisters". This option demands that we recognize the implications of the universal destination of the world's goods. It also calls for "an appreciation of the immense dignity of the poor in the light of our deepest convictions as believers. It is quite clear that "this option is in fact an ethical imperative essential for effectively attaining the common good".[69]

4. Justice between the generations. The notion of the common good is applicable to future generations. As Pope Francis insists: We can no longer speak of sustainable development apart from intergenerational solidarity. Intergenerational solidarity is not optional, but rather a basic question of justice, since the world we have received also belongs to those who will follow us. The Portuguese bishops have called upon us to acknowledge this obligation of justice. "The environment is part of a logic of receptivity. It is on loan to each generation, which must then hand it on to the next". An integral ecology is marked by this broader vision.[70]

We need to honestly face the question: What kind world do we want to leave to those who come after us?

V. Lines of Approach and Action

In this Chapter Five Pope Francis discusses a five-fold dialogue in order to find an effective solution to our ecological crisis.

1. International Dialogue on the Environment

Since the middle of the last century "there has been a growing conviction that our planet is a homeland and that humanity is one people living in a common home". Pope Francis spells out the implications of such a conviction: "An interdependent world not only makes us more conscious of the negative effects of certain lifestyles and models of production and consumption which affect us all; more importantly, it motivates us to ensure that solutions are proposed from a global perspective, and not simply to defend the interests of a few countries. Interdependence obliges us to think of one world with a common plan".[71]

The Pope points out that significant advances have been made by the ecological movement in recent years because of the efforts of many organizations of the civil society. As a result of their work environmental questions have found a place on public agendas. "This notwithstanding, recent world summits on the environment have not lived up to expectations because due to lack of political will, they were unable to reach meaningful and effective global agreements on the environment".[72]

However Pope Francis singles out two international agreements as positive steps:

a. The 1992 Earth Summit in Rio de Janeiro is worth mentioning. It proclaimed that "human beings are at the centre of concerns for sustainable development".[73] Echoing the 1972 Stockholm Declaration, it enshrined international cooperation to care for the ecosystem of the entire earth, the obligation of those who cause pollution to assume its costs, and the duty to assess the environmental impact of given projects and works. It set the goal of limiting greenhouse gas concentration in the atmosphere, in an effort to reverse the trend of global warming. It also drew up an agenda with an action plan and a convention on biodiversity, and stated principles regarding forests. Although the summit was a real step forward, and prophetic for its time, its accords have been poorly implemented, due to the lack of suitable mechanisms for oversight, periodic review and penalties in cases of non-compliance. The principles which it proclaimed still await an efficient and flexible means of practical implementation.[74]

b. The Basel Convention on hazardous wastes, with its system of reporting, standards and controls. There is also the binding Convention on international trade in endangered species of wild fauna and flora, which includes onsite visits for verifying effective compliance. Thanks to the Vienna Convention for the protection of the ozone layer and its implementation through the Montreal Protocol and amendments, the problem of the layer's thinning seems to have entered a phase of resolution.[75]

There are many areas of concern that must be urgently addressed by the international community.

a. "We know that technology based on the use of highly polluting fossil fuels especially coal, but also oil and, to a lesser degree, gas – needs to be progressively replaced without delay"[76] We have to develop widely accessible sources of renewable energy. For this there is an urgent need of international cooperation, especially to help poorer countries to meet the cost of this energy transition.
b. Protection of biodiversity and tackling issues related the desertification. "With regard to climate change, the advances have been regrettably few. Reducing greenhouse gases requires honesty, courage and responsibility, above all on the part of those countries which are more powerful and pollute the most".[77]
c. Some strategies for lowering pollutant gas emissions call for the internationalization of environmental costs, which would risk imposing on countries with fewer resources burdensome commitments to reducing emissions comparable to those of the more industrialized countries. Imposing such measures penalizes those countries most in need of development.[78]
d. Global regulatory norms are needed to impose obligations and prevent unacceptable actions, for example, when powerful companies dump contaminated waste or offshore polluting industries in other countries.
e. There is urgent need of a system of governance of the oceans. As the Pope has observed: "The growing problem of marine waste and the protection of the open seas represent particular challenges. What is

needed, in effect, is an agreement on systems of governance of the whole range of so –called "global commons".[79]

f. There is need for an effective international authority to enact and implement stringent ecological measures. Here the Pope quotes with approval the words of Pope Benedict XVI:" To manage the global economy; to revive economies hit by the crisis; to avoid any deterioration of the present crisis and the greater imbalances that would result; to bring about integral and timely disarmament, food security and peace; to guarantee the protection of the environment and to regulate migration: for all this, there is urgent need of a true world political authority, as my predecessor Blessed John XXIII indicated some years ago".[80]

2. Dialogue for New National and Local Policies

States should take responsibility for dealing with questions related to the environment and economic development. Because of the possibility of "the misuse of human abilities, individual states can no longer ignore their responsibility for planning, coordination, oversight and enforcement within their respective borders". As the Pope points out, "One authoritative source of oversight and coordination is the law, which lays down rules for admissible conduct in the light of the common good. At present there is a growing jurisprudence dealing with the reduction of pollution by business activities. "But political and institutional frameworks do not exist simply to avoid bad practice, but also to promote best practice, to stimulate creativity in seeking new solutions and to encourage individual or group initiatives".[81]

Politicians are concerned with immediate results, supported by consumerist interests. Hence they will go in for short – term growth. Because of electoral interests governments are reluctant to upset the public with measures which could adversely affect their daily life. "True statecraft is manifest when, in difficult times, we uphold high principles and think of the long term common good. Political powers do not find it easy to assume this duty in the work of nation-building".[82]

There are places where cooperatives are being formed to exploit renewal sources of energy which ensure local self-sufficiency. It is clear that, while the present world order is powerless to assume its responsibilities, local individuals and groups can make a real difference. "They are able to instil a greater sense of responsibility, a strong sense of community, a readiness to protect others, a spirit of creativity and a deep love for the land. They are also concerned about what they will eventually leave to their children and grandchildren. These values are deeply rooted in indigenous peoples".[83]

A lot can be done on the local level if there are capable and committed leadership. "Political activity on the local level could also be directed to modifying consumption, developing an economy of waste disposal and recycling, protecting certain species and planning a diversified agriculture and the rotation of crops". As the Pope observes: "New forms of cooperation and community organization can be encouraged in order to defend the interests of small producers and preserve local ecosystems from destruction".[84]

Besides, we need to be aware of the fact that policies related to climate change and the protection of the environment will take time to produce tangible results. That is why continuity of leadership is necessary. Bold leaders are needed to ensure continuity: "But if they are courageous, they will attest to their God-given dignity and leave behind a testimony of selfless responsibility. A healthy politics is sorely needed, capable of reforming and coordinating institutions, promoting best practices and overcoming undue pressure and bureaucratic inertia".[85] However we have to remember "that even the best mechanisms can break down when there are no worthy goals and values, or a genuine and profound humanism to serve as the basis of a noble and generous society".[86]

3. Dialogue and Transparency in Decision-Making

How is a community to decide whether a business proposition or the proposal for a particular policy, plan or programme is viable from the point of view of its environmental impact? An honest assessment of its impact on the environment should be made. "It should be part of the process from the beginning, and be carried out in a way which is interdisciplinary, transparent and free of all economic or political pressure. It should be linked to a study of working conditions and possible effects on people's physical and mental health, on the local economy and on public safety. A consensus should always be reached between the different stakeholders, who can offer a variety of approaches, solutions and alternatives. The local population should have a special place at the table; they are concerned about their own future and that of their children, and can consider goals transcending immediate economic interest.[87]

4. Politics and Economy in "Dialogue for Human Fulfilment". Here the Pope makes three observations.
    a. Politics must not be subject to the economy, nor should the economy be subject to the dictates of an efficiency-driven paradigm of technocracy. Today, in view of the common good, there is urgent need for politics and economics to enter into a frank dialogue in the service of life, especially human life. Saving banks at any cost, making the public pay the price, foregoing a firm commitment to reviewing and reforming the entire system, only reaffirms the absolute power of a financial system, a power which has no future and will only give rise to new crises after a slow, costly and only apparent recovery.[88]
    b. A path of productive development, which is more creative and better directed, could correct the present disparity between excessive technological investment in consumption and insufficient investment

in resolving urgent problems facing the human family. It could generate intelligent and profitable ways of reusing, revamping and recycling, and it could also improve the energy efficiency of cities. Productive diversification offers the fullest possibilities to human ingenuity to create and innovate, while at the same time protecting the environment and creating more sources of employment. Such creativity would be a worthy expression of our most noble human qualities, for we would be striving intelligently, boldly and responsibly to promote a sustainable and equitable development within the context of a broader concept of quality of life.[89]

c. That is why time has come to accept decreased growth in some parts of the world, in order to provide resources for other places to experience healthy growth. Benedict XVI has said that "technologically advanced societies must be prepared to encourage more sober lifestyles, while reducing their energy consumption and improving its efficiency".[90]

5. Religions in Dialogue with Science

The Pope begins this section by pointing out that empirical science, precisely because of its own methodology, cannot offer a "complete explanation of life, the interplay of all creatures and the whole of reality". If we reason only within the confines of empirical science no room would be left for aesthetic sensibility, poetry, or even reason's ability to grasp the ultimate meaning and purpose of things.[91] Here the Pope goes on to add:

Religious classics can prove meaningful in every age; they have an enduring power to open new horizons… Is it reasonable and enlightened to dismiss certain writings simply because they arose in the context of religious belief?[92]

By way of concluding this chapter Pope Francis makes some perceptive comments:

> The majority of people living on our planet profess to be believers. This should spur religions to dialogue among themselves for the sake of protecting nature, defending the poor, and building networks of respect and fraternity. Dialogue among the various sciences is likewise needed, since each can tend to become enclosed in its own language, while specialization leads to a certain isolation and the absolutization of its own field of knowledge. This prevents us from confronting environmental problems effectively. An open and respectful dialogue is also needed between the various ecological movements, among which ideological conflicts are not infrequently encountered. The gravity of the ecological crisis demands that we all look to the common good, embarking on a path of dialogue which demands patience, self-discipline and generosity, always keeping in mind that "realities are greater than ideas".[93]

VI Ecological Education and Spirituality

Pope Francis insists that many things have to change, especially we human beings, if we are to deal constructively with the ecological crisis.

According to the Pope: We lack an awareness of our common origin, of our mutual belonging, and of a future to be shared with everyone. This basic awareness would enable the development of new convictions, attitudes and forms of life. A great cultural, spiritual and educational challenge stands before us, and it will demand that we set out on the long path of renewal.[94]

1. Towards a New Lifestyle

A major problem today is compulsive consumerism which leads to needless buying and spending. As the Pope points out: When people become " self – centred and self-enclosed, their greed increases. The emptier a person's heart is, the more he or she needs things to buy, own and consume. It becomes almost impossible to accept the limits imposed by reality. In this horizon a genuine sense of the common good also disappears.[95]

The Pope is convinced that we are capable of a change of lifestyle: We are able to take an honest look at ourselves, to acknowledge our deep dissatisfaction, and to embark on new paths to authentic freedom. No system can completely suppress our openness to what is good, true and beautiful, or our God-given ability to respond to his grace at work deep in our hearts. I appeal to everyone throughout the world not to forget this dignity which is ours.[96]

A change in lifestyle will exert pressure on those who wield political, economic or social power. Consumer movements achieve this by boycotting certain products. They succeed in changing the way businesses operate, forcing them to consider their impact on the environment and their patterns of production. When social pressure affects their profit, businesses will be forced to produce differently. There is need to develop a greater sense of social responsibility on the part of consumers. ? The Pope draws the conclusion: "Environmental degradation challenges us to examine our lifestyle".[97]

The Pope concludes this section with some memorable words: "Disinterested concern for others, and the rejection of every form of self-centredness and self-absorption, are essential if we truly wish to care for our brothers and sisters and for the natural environment. These attitudes also attune us to the moral imperative of assessing the impact of our every action and personal decision on the world around us. If we can overcome individualism, we will truly be able to develop a different lifestyle and bring about significant changes in society".[98]

2. Educating for the Covenant between Humanity and the Environment.

A deep awareness of today's cultural and ecological crisis should lead to the acquisition of new habits. Yet brought up in a consumerist culture people find it difficult to give up what the market places before them. There are, however, many young people who have a new ecological sensitivity and a generous spirit, but because of the influence of the prevalent consumerist culture they find it difficult to cultivate new habits. This is an educational challenge for us.[99]

As the Pope has observed:

> Environmental education has broadened its goals. Whereas in the beginning it was mainly centred on scientific information, consciousness-raising and the prevention of environmental risks, it tends now to include a critique of the "myths" of a modernity grounded in a utilitarian mindset (individualism, unlimited progress, competition, consumerism, the unregulated market). It seeks also to restore the various levels of ecological equilibrium, establishing harmony within ourselves, with others, with nature and other living creatures, and with God. Environmental education should facilitate making the leap towards the transcendent which gives ecological ethics its deepest meaning. It needs educators capable of developing an ethics of ecology, and helping people, through effective pedagogy, to grow in solidarity, responsibility and compassionate care.[100]

There is a variety of settings where environmental education can take place: at school, in families, in the media, in catechesis etc. Family is the most important of these. It helps to create a culture of shared life and respect for our surroundings. As the Pope has pointed out: "Good education plants seeds when we are young, and these continue to bear fruit throughout life".[101]

3. Ecological Conversion

The Pope begins this section by stating that the Christian tradition should help to develop a spirituality that "motivates us to a more passionate concern for the protection of our world".[102]

For this we need an "ecological conversion", "whereby the effects of our encounter with Jesus Christ become evident in our relationship with the world around us".[103] The Pope spells out the concrete implications of such a conversion:

This conversion calls for a number of attitudes which together foster a spirit of generous care, full of tenderness. First, it entails gratitude and gratuitousness, a recognition that the world is God's loving gift, and that we are called quietly to imitate his generosity in self-sacrifice and good works: "Do not let your left hand know what your right hand is doing… and your Father who sees in secret will reward you" (Mt 6:3-4). It also entails a loving awareness that we are not disconnected from the rest of creatures, but joined in a splendid universal communion. As believers, we do not look at the world from without but from within, conscious of the bonds with which the Father has linked us to all beings. By developing our individual, God-given capacities, an ecological conversion can inspire us to greater creativity and enthusiasm in resolving the world's problems and in offering ourselves to God "as a living sacrifice, holy and acceptable" (Rom 12:1). We do not understand our superiority as a reason for personal glory or irresponsible dominion, but rather as a different capacity which, in its turn, entails a serious responsibility stemming from our faith.[104]

4. Joy and Peace

What kind of a lifestyle will bring us a lot of peace and joy? This is the Pope's answer to this question:

Christian spirituality proposes an alternative understanding of the quality of life, and encourages a prophetic and contemplative lifestyle, one capable of deep enjoyment free of the obsession with consumption. We need to take up an ancient lesson, found in different religious traditions and also in the Bible. It is the conviction that "less is more". A constant flood of new consumer goods can baffle the heart and prevent us from cherishing each thing and each moment. To be serenely present to each reality, however small it may be, opens us to much greater horizons of understanding and personal fulfilment. Christian spirituality proposes a growth marked by moderation and the capacity to be happy with little. It is a return to that simplicity which allows us to stop and appreciate the small things, to be grateful for the opportunities which life affords us, to be spiritually detached from what we possess, and not to succumb to sadness for what we lack.[105]

Pope Francis makes three more observations on the topic of Joy and Peace:

1) "Happiness means knowing how to limit some needs which only diminish us, and being open to many different possibilities which life can offer".[106]
2) "No one can cultivate a sober and satisfying life without being at peace with him or herself... Inner peace is closely related to care for ecology and for the common good because lived out authentically, it is reflected in a balanced lifestyle together with a capacity for wonder which takes us to a deeper understanding of life".[107]
3) An integral ecology includes taking time to recover a serene harmony with creation, reflecting on our lifestyle and our ideals, and contemplating the Creator who lives among us and surrounds us, whose presence "must not be contrived but found, uncovered".[108]

5. Civic and Political love

In this section the Pope makes two significant observations:

1. We must regain the conviction that we need one another, that we have a shared responsibility for others and the world, and that being good and decent is worth it. We have had enough of immorality and the mockery of ethics, goodness, faith and honesty. It is time to acknowledge that light-hearted superficiality has done us no good. When the foundations of social life are corroded, what ensues are battles over conflicting

interests, new forms of violence and brutality, and obstacles to the growth of a genuine culture of care for the environment.[109]

2. Social love is the key to authentic development: "In order to make society more human, more worthy of the human person, love in social life – political, economic and cultural – must be given renewed value, becoming the constant and highest norm for all activity. In this framework, along with the importance of little everyday gestures, social love moves us to devise larger strategies to halt environmental degradation and to encourage a "culture of care" which permeates all of society.[110]

6. The Trinity and the Relationship Between Creatures

All creation is the work of the Triune God. The Trinity has left its mark on all creation. Hence each creature bears in itself a specifically Trinitarian structure. Hence we are invited to see reality in a Trinitarian way. Besides, as the Pope points out: The divine Persons are subsistent relations, and the world, created according to the divine model, is a web of relationships. Creatures tend towards God, and in turn it is proper to every living being to tend towards other things, so that throughout the universe we can find any number of constant and secretly interwoven relationships". This helps us to marvel at the innumerable connections that exist among creatures, but also discover a key to our own growth.[111]

7. Not Taking Away the Joy of Our Hope

The Pope ends the Encyclical on a very hopeful note:

> At the end, we will find ourselves face to face with the infinite beauty of God (cf. 1 Cor 13:12), and be able to read with admiration and happiness the mystery of the universe, which with us will share in unending plenitude. Even now we are journeying towards the Sabbath of eternity, the new Jerusalem, towards our common home in heaven. Jesus says: "I make all things new" (Rev 21:5). Eternal life will be a shared experience of awe, in which each creature, resplendently transfigured, will take its rightful place and have something to give those poor men and women who will have been liberated once and for all.[112]

Now united with all creatures we are journeying through the earth seeking God. "Let us sing as we go". "May our struggles and our concern for this planet never a take away the joy of our hope".[113]

The Pope concludes *Laudato Si'* with two prayers for the earth – one inter-religious and the other Christian.

VII Reflections

a. *Laudato Si'* is unique in the history of papal encyclicals. While several recent Popes have touched upon the environmental problem in their writings, Pope Francis is the first Pope to devote a whole encyclical to the discussion of the ecological crisis which we are facing today.

b. *Laudato Si'* deals with the ecology comprehensively. It begins with an examination of the manifestations of the global ecological crisis. It goes on to enquire into the causes of this crisis. Then it develops some theological perspectives on ecology. It further spells out lines of approach and action in order to deal with this crisis effectively. It also discusses the spirituality that can motivate us to take concrete steps to protect the environment and indicates the need for a well planned ecological education. All in all this is a rich and inspiring document.

c. The way Pope Francis speaks of Saint Francis of Assissi is quite thought provoking:

> I believe that Saint Francis is the example par excellence of care for the vulnerable and of an integral ecology lived out joyfully and authentically. He is the patron saint of all who study and work in the area of ecology, and he is also much loved by non-Christians. He was particularly concerned for God's creation and for the poor and outcast. He loved, and was deeply loved for his joy, his generous self-giving, his openheartedness. He was a mystic and a pilgrim who lived in simplicity and in wonderful harmony with God, with others, with nature and with himself. He shows us just how inseparable the bond is between concern for nature, justice for the poor, commitment to society, and interior peace.[114]

d. The Pope calls for a genuine conversion to the world:

> For this reason, the ecological crisis is also a summons to a profound interior conversion. It must be said that some committed and prayerful Christians, with the excuse of realism and pragmatism, tend to ridicule expressions of concern for the environment. Others are passive; they choose not to change their habits and thus become inconsistent. So what they all need is an "ecological conversion", whereby the effects of their encounter with Jesus Christ become evident in their relationship with the world around them. Living our vocation to be protectors of God's handiwork is essential to a life of virtue; it is not an optional or a secondary aspect of our Christian experience.[115]

e. Pope Francis makes an insightful comment that the ecological crisis and the social crisis are one and the same: "We are faced not with two separate crisis, one environmental and the other social, but rather with one complex crisis which is both social and environmental. Strategies for a solution demand an integrated approach to combating poverty, restoring dignity to the excluded, and at the same time protecting nature".[116]

f. As has been pointed out: "Thus the encyclical brings to the fore many important social aspects of human life which include, among others, the critique of technology, the criticism of naïve faith in the virtues of the market economy which claims to offer solutions to our collective problems, the invitation to seek other ways of understanding the economy and progress, the dignity of every human being, the need for sincere and honest debates in which all stakeholders especially the poorest and the least are represented and have a say, responsibility both in domestic and international politics, the connection between policy change and change in lifestyle and the contribution of education and spirituality.[117]

g. I have the impression that *Laudato Si'* is a bit too long. Hence it might discourage people from reading and studying it. But all those who have the courage to make a serious study of this Encyclical will be greatly enriched.

Notes

1. *Laudato Si'* (Hereafter *LS*), n. 1
2. *Ibid.* n. 10
3. *Ibid*
4. Paul VI, *Octogesima Adveniens*, Rome, 1971, n. 21
5. John Paul II, *Centesimus Annus*, Rome, 1991, n. 38
6. Benedict XVI, *Caritas in Veritate*, Rome, 2009, n. 51
7. Ecumenieal, Patriarch Bartholomew, Address in Santa Barbara, 8 November 1997
8. Lecture at the Monastery of Utstein, 20 June 2012
9. *LS* n. 14
10. *LS* n. 19
11. See *LS* 20
12. *LS* 23
13. *LS* 24
14. *LS* 25
15. *LS* 28
16. *LS* 30
17. *LS* 32
18. *LS* 34
19. *LS* 44
20. *LS* 48
21. *LS* 49
22. *LS* 52
23. As quoted in *LS* n. 61
24. *LS* n. 101
25. *LS* n. 103
26. *LS* n. 105
27. *LS* n. 107
28. *LS* n. *108*
29. *LS* n. 110

30. *LS* n. 112
31. *LS* n, 114
32. *LS* n. *116*
33. *LS* n. 118
34. *LS* n. 115
35. *LS* n.122
36. *LS* n. 63
37. *LS* n. 62
38. *LS* n. 64
39. *LS* n. *65*
40. *Ibid*
41. *LS* n. *66*
42. *LS* n. 67
43. *LS* n. 68
44. *LS* n. 69
45. *LS* n. 70
46. *LS* n. *75*
47. *LS* n. 77
48. *LS n. 78*
49. *LS* n. 81
50. *LS* n. 85
51. *LS* n. 86
52. *LS* n. 89
53. *LS* n. *92*
54. *LS* n. 93
55. *LS* n. 95
56. *LS* n. 98
57. *LS* n. 138
58. *LS* n. 139
59. *LS* n. 141
60. *LS* n. 142
61. *LS* n. 143
62. *LS* n. 144
63. *LS* n. 145
64. *LS* n. 147
65. *LS* n. 152
66. *LS* n, 153
67. *LS* n. 156
68. *LS* n. 157
69. *LS* n. 158
70. *LS* n. 159
71. *LS* n. 164
72. *LS* n. 166
73. *LS* n. *167*
74. *LS* n. *Ibid*
75. *LS* n. *168*
76. *LS* n. 165
77. *LS* n. 169
78. *LS* n. *170*
79. *LS* n. *174*

80. *LS* n. 175
81. *LS* n. 177
82. LS n. 178
83. *LS* n. *179*
84. *LS* n. 180
85. *LS* n. 169
86. *LS ibid*
87. *LS* n. 183
88. *LS*n. 189
89. *LS* n. 192
90. *LS* n. 193
91. *LS* n. 199
92. *Ibid*
93. *LS* n. 201
94. *LS* n. 202
95. *LS* n. 204
96. *LS* n. 205
97. *LS* n. 206
98. *LS* n. 208
99. *LS* n. 209
100. *LS* n. 210
101. *LS* n. 213
102. *LS* n. 216
103. *LS* n. 217
104. *LS* n. 220
105. *LS* n. 222
106. *LS* n. 223
107. *LS* n. 225
108. *Ibid*
109. *LS* n. 229
110. *LS* n. 231
111. *LS* n. 240
112. *LS* n. 243
113. *LS* n. 244
114. *LS* n. 110
115. *LS* n. 217
116. *LS* n. 139
117. N.A. Irudayadasan, "Striking a poetic chord with Love of Nature and the Poor: Reflections on *Laudato Si*" in *Asian Journal of Rel. Studies,* 60 (Nov. 2019) 6, p.11.

15

THE JOY OF LOVE

Discussion of a Recent Papal Exhortation

On 19 March 2016 Pope Francis issued the Post-Synodal Apostolic Exhortation *Amoris Laetitia* which deals with marriage and the family. It seeks "to gather the contributions of two recent synods on the Family (held in Rome in 2014 and 2015), while adding other considerations as an aid to reflection, dialogue and pastoral practice, and as a help and encouragement to families in their daily commitments and challenges."[1] Basing himself on the Synod Fathers the Pope asserts that, for all the many signs of crisis in the institution of marriage, "the desire to marry and to form a family remains vibrant, especially among young people, and this is an inspiration to the Church."[2] As a response to this desire, "the Christian proclamation on the family is good news indeed."[3] The tone of the Exhortation is quite positive. It points out that "families are not a problem; they are first and foremost an opportunity."[4]

Since the Exhortation deals with a wide variety of questions, it is invariably quite long (68000 words). Hence, it is not possible for me in this paper to discuss all the rich ideas and insights found in this document. What I endeavour to do is to highlight its most significant ideas and insights and reflect on them. It is my fond hope that such an approach will help readers to gain an adequate understanding of this remarkable Exhortation.

This paper begins with a brief description of the concrete situation of families today as well as the challenges marriage and the family face. It goes on to develop some theological perspectives on the topic. Then it discusses love in marriage and children as the fruit of this love. It also deals with some of the steps that could be taken in order to impart quality education to the children. Then it seeks to develop some pastoral perspectives on marriage and the family and discuss some aspects of concrete pastoral care in the context of the problems and difficulties which marriage and family face today. After this there is a brief treatment of the spirituality of marriage and the family. The paper will conclude with some evaluative comments on the Exhortation

I. The Situation of Marriage and Family in the world today

Sometime back the Spanish bishops pointed out that families have come to enjoy greater freedom "through an equitable distribution of duties, responsibilities and tasks" and that a "greater emphasis on personal communication between the spouses helps to make family life more humane."[5]

1. Pope Francis highlights some of the positive elements in the situation of marriage and family today:

   > We must be grateful that most people do value family relationships that are permanent and marked by mutual respect. They appreciate the Church's efforts to offer guidance and counselling in areas related to growth in love, overcoming conflict and raising children. Many are touched by the power of grace experienced in sacramental Reconciliation and in the Eucharist, grace that helps them to face the challenges of marriage and the family. In some countries, especially in various parts of Africa, secularism has not weakened certain traditional values, and marriages forge a strong bond between two wider families, with clearly defined structures for dealing with problems and conflicts. Nowadays we are grateful too for the witness of marriages that have not only proved lasting, but also fruitful and loving.[6]

2. But there are many factors that create serious difficulties for marriage and the family life. There is the unbridled growth of extreme individualism "which weakens family bonds and ends up by considering each member of the family as an isolated unit."[7] This often leads "to the idea that one's personality is shaped by his or her desires, which are considered absolute". The prevailing culture is overly individualistic and is caught up with possessions and pleasures. This leads "to intolerance and hostilities in families."[8] Closely related to this is the emphasis placed on a personalism which opts for authenticity as opposed to mere conformity". But there are two sides to personalism. On the one hand it can foster spontaneity and a better use of people's talents. On the other hand it can, if not properly directed, lead to "attitudes of constant suspicion, fear of commitment, self-centredness and arrogance."[9]

   Freedom, too, becomes dangerous to marriage and family life. It is true that freedom "makes it possible to plan our lives and to make the most of ourselves".

But if people have no noble goals and personal discipline freedom easily degenerates into an inability to give oneself generously to others. In many countries a growing number of people are choosing to live alone or simply to spent time together without cohabiting.[10]

Economic factors also can cause problems for marriage and the family. Sometimes they prevent some people from getting married. Others postpone marriage for lack of dignified or affordable housing.

The weakening of faith and religious practice has a negative impact on families. Often this leads to a feeling of loneliness "arising out of the absence of God in a person's life and the fragility of relationships". Some families experience a sense of powerlessness in the face of socio-cultural realities which often oppress them. They also feel helpless and abandoned because of a lack of interest and attention on the part of public institutions. The social order sometimes impacts the families negatively leading to a "demographic crisis". It has become difficult to raise children, to welcome new life and to treat older persons with respect and love. All this creates emotional problems which sometimes lead to the outbreak of violence.[11]

It must be admitted that the Church has often failed to provide inspiration and guidance to married couples and families to cope with the challenges and difficulties of marriage and family life in the modern world. The Church has to become aware that no useful purpose is served by simply condemning present-day evils in marriage and family life. What it has failed to do is to "make a more generous effort to present the reasons and motivations for choosing marriage and the family, and in this way help men and women better to respond to the grace that God offers them."[12] As the Pope has pointed out: Besides, the Church has failed to provide meaningful guidance to young married couples, understanding their timetables, their way of thinking and their concrete concerns. Sometimes, it has placed before them a far too abstract and well-nigh artificial theological ideal of marriage, far removed from the concrete situations and practical possibilities of real families. "This excessive idealization, especially when we have failed to inspire trust in God's grace, has not helped to make marriage more desirable and attractive, but quite the opposite."[13]

We have to realize that merely by stressing doctrinal, bioethical and moral issues without encouraging people to be open to grace we are not providing sufficient assistance to families, strengthening the marriage bond and giving meaning to marital life. What we need to do is "to present marriage more as a dynamic path to personal development and fulfilment than a lifelong burden."[14] We also have to respect the consciences of people who are trying their best to respond to the gospel with their limitations, and are capable of making a sincere discernment in the complex situation of today. "We have been called to form consciences, and not to replace them", the Pope reminds us.[15]

The State, too, often fails to assist families. It does not fulfil its duty to pass laws and create work in order to ensure the future of young people and help them to realize their plan of forming a family."[16] Sometimes the State forcibly intervenes "in favour of contraception, sterilization and even abortion."[17]

The presence of the elderly in families evokes a two-fold response. There are many families which welcome them, treat them with love and respect and regard them as a blessing. But there are other families which are not happy and tend to look upon then as a burden. It is true that taking care of the elderly often puts a strain on their children. The elderly are sometimes unfairly exploited for economic reasons.[18] It is a matter of joy that Church institutions take care of a large number of people who are old and infirm.

Finally there are a good number of children who are born outside of wedlock. Many of them grow up with only one of the parents. The sexual exploitation of children is a sad reality in the present-day world. What is quite shocking is that it often happens where children should be most safe – in families, schools, communities and Christian institutions. It is also to be noted that the phenomenon of "street-children" is on the rise, especially in large cities.

Towards the end of the chapter the Pope speaks of the challenges that marriage and family life face today. I shall now discuss them."

First there is the challenge of raising children. Often parents come home exhausted and are too tired to talk. Then sometimes it is not possible for families to share a common meal. In the world today there are many distractions, especially an addiction to television. All this makes it difficult for parents to hand on the faith to children. Families often face severe stress and are so preoccupied with securing a future that they are not able to enjoy the present. This is part of a broad cultural problem made all the more difficult by fears about stable employment, finance and the future of children.

There is also the challenge of drug, alcoholism, and other addictions which cause untold suffering and often lead to the breakup of many families. As a result of this breakdown families are torn apart, the young are uprooted and the elderly are abandoned. Thus we have the phenomenon of children who are orphans of living parents, and adolescents and young adults confused and unsupported. It is true that violence within families breed new forms of social aggression.[19] As has been pointed out:

This is often the case with families where communication is lacking, defensive attitudes predominate, the members are not supportive of one another, family activities that encourage participation are absent, the parental relationship is frequently conflictual and violent, and relationships between parents and children are marked by hostility. Violence within the family is a breeding-ground of resentment and hatred in the most basic human relationships.[20]

II. Theological Perspectives

Pope Francis develops some theological perspectives, based on Sacred scripture and the teaching of the Magisterium.

1. Biblical Basis

As Genesis says: "God created humankind in his image, in the image of God he created them: male and female he created them" (Gen 1:27). It is remarkable that the image of God here refers to the couple.

A couple's fruitful love becomes an image for understanding and describing the Christian vision of the Trinity. For the triune God is not a solitude, but a communion of persons. Pope John Paul II points out: In his deepest mystery our God "is not a solitude, but a family, for he has within himself fatherhood, sonship and the essence of the family which is love. That love, in the divine family, is the Holy Spirit."[21] Thus, the family is related to God's very being.

Genesis in chapter two paints the picture of man who feels lonely and is in search of "a helper fit for him", who is able to alleviate the solitude which he feels amid the animals and the world around him. God now fashions the woman from the rib he took from the man and brings her to the man. And the man is quite pleased and says: "This at last is bone of my bones and flesh of my flesh; this one shall be called woman" (Gen 2:23).[22]

Genesis goes on to add:"Therefore a man leaves his father and mother and clings to his wife and they become one flesh" (Gen 2:24) Jesus quotes this verse approvingly (Matt.18:5).

In the New Testament Paul speaks of the church in the house of Aquila and Prisca (see 1 Cor 16:9: Rom 16:5). Reflecting on the idea of the domestic church Pope Francis observes:

> A family's living space could turn into a domestic church, a setting for the Eucharist, the presence of Christ seated at its table. We can never forget the image found in the book of revelation, where the Lord says:" Behold, I stand at the door and knock: if any one hears my voice and opens the door, I will come in to him and eat with him and he with me". Here we see a home filled with the presence of God, common prayer and every blessing. This is the meaning of the conclusion of Psalm 128: "Thus shall the man be blessed who fears the Lord. The Lord blesses you from Zion! "(Ps 128: 4-5).[23]

The Bible looks upon the family as the place where children are instructed in the faith. This is clear from the description of the Passover (see Ex 12:26-27; Deut 6:20-25). One of the Psalms speaks of the proclamation of the faith within the families:

> All that we have heard and known, that our ancestors have told us, we will not hide them from their children: we will tell to the coming

> generation the glorious deeds of the Lord, and his might, and the wonders that he has wrought. He established a decree in Jacob, and appointed a law in Israel, which he commanded our fathers to teach to their children; that the next generation might know them, the children yet unborn, and rise up and tell them to their children (Ps 78:3-6).

The biblical sage often reminds parents of their serious responsibility for the work of educating children (Prov 3:11-12:6:20-22; 23:13-14; 24:17). Children are called upon to observe the commandment: "Honour your father and mother" (Ex 20:12). Here the verb to honour has to do with the fulfilment of family and social commitments; these are not to be disregarded under the prentnce of religious motives" (Mtt.7:11-13). According to Jesus Sirach:" Whoever honours his father atones for his sins, and whoever glorifies his mother is like one who lays up treasure" (Sir 3:3-4).

In the societies of ancient Near East people used to look upon children as family property or as people who have no rights. However, Jesus presents children as teachers: "Truly I say to you, unless you change and become like children, you will never enter the kingdom of heaven, Whoever becomes humble like this child is the greatest in the kingdom of heaven" (Matt 18:3-4).

Rejecting the views of those who looked upon marriage as evil the New Testament teaches "that everything created by God is good and nothing is to be rejected" (1 Tim 4:4). Marriage is a gift from the Lord (1Cor 7:7). Precisely because it is God's gift, it has to be appreciated and protected by humans: "Let marriage be held in honour by all, and let the marriage bed be undefiled (Heb 13:4).

Jesus stoutly defended the indissolubility of marriage. As we read in Mark's gospel Jesus clearly stated: "Whoever divorces his wife and marries another commits adultery against her: and if she divorces her husband and marries another, she commits adultery" (Mk 10:11-12). But the Pharisees who questioned Jesus about divorce asked: "Why then did Moses command us to give a certificate of dismissal and to divorce her" (Matt 19:7). Jesus explained: "It was because you were so hard–hearted that Moses allowed you to divorce your wives, but from the beginning it was not so." Here, Pope Francis makes a pertinent comment: "the indissolubility of marriage –'what God has joined together, let no man put asunder' (Mtt 19:6)- should not be viewed as a 'yoke' imposed on humanity, but as a 'gift' granted to those who are joined in marriage..... God's indulgent love always accompanies our human journey; through grace, it heals and transforms hardened hearts, leading them back to the beginning through the way of the cross. The Gospels clearly present the example of Jesus who....proclaimed the meaning of marriage as the fullness of revelation that restores God's original plan" (cf. Matt 19:3).[24]

The covenant of love and fidelity lived by the Holy Family sheds light on the principle (love) that brings every family into existence and enables it better to face the vicissitudes of life. For this reason every family though suffering from some weakness can become a light in the darkness of the world. As Pope Paul VI stated in an address at Nazareth: "Nazareth teaches us the meaning of family life, its loving communion, and its simple and austere beauty, its sacred and inviolable character. May it teach how sweet and irreplaceable is its training, how fundamental and incomparable its role in the social order."[25]

2. The Teaching of the Magisterium

In its Pastoral Constitution on the Church in the Modern World Vatican II sought "to promote 'the dignity of marriage and the family" (nos.47-52). The Constitution described "marriage as an intimate partnership of life and love" (n.48), placing love at the centre of married life. "True love between husband and wife involves mutual self-giving, includes and integrates the sexual and affective dimensions in accordance with God's plan" (nos.48-49). Christ the Lord makes himself present to the Christian spouses in the sacrament of marriage (n.48), and remains with them. In the incarnation he assumes human love, purifies it and brings it to fulfilment. By the gift of the Holy Spirit, he bestows on the spouses the capacity to live that love permeating every part of their lives of faith, hope and charity, By means of a special grace the spouses build up the body of Christ and forms a domestic church "so that the Church, in order fully to understand her mystery, looks to the Christian family, which manifests her in a real way."[26]

In his encyclical *Humanae Vitae* Paul VI pointed out the intrinsic bond between the conjugal love and the generation of life: "Married love requires of husband and wife the full awareness of their obligations in the matter of responsible parenthood, which today, rightly enough, is much insisted upon, but which at the same time must be rightly understood.... The exercise of responsible parenthood requires that husband and wife, keeping a right order of priorities, recognize their own duties towards God, themselves, their families and human society."[27]

John Paul II spoke of the family as "the way of the Church". While discussing conjugal love he described "how spouses, in their mutual love, receive the gift of the Spirit of Christ and live their call to holiness".

As Pope Francis explains:

> The sacrament of marriage is not a social convention, an empty ritual or merely the outward sign of a commitment. The sacrament is a gift given for the sanctification and salvation of the spouses, since "their mutual belonging is a real representation, through the sacramental sign, of the same relationship between Christ and the Church. The married couple is therefore a permanent reminder for the Church of what took place on the cross: they are for one another and for their children witnesses of the salvation in which they share through the sacrament.[28]

The fact that marriage is a sacrament gives depth and meaning to the sexual relations between the husband and wife. In the words of the Pope:

Sexual union, lovingly experienced and sanctified by the sacrament, is in turn a path of growth in the life of grace for the couple. It is the "nuptial mystery". The meaning and value of their physical union is expressed in the words of consent, in which they accepted and offered themselves each to the other, in order to share their lives completely. Those words give meaning to the sexual relationship and free it from ambiguity. More generally, the common life of husband and wife, the entire network of relations that they build with their children and the world around them, will be steeped in and strengthened by the grace of the sacrament.[29]

It is the constant teaching of the Church that the conjugal union, by its nature, is ordered to procreation. The child who is born "does not come from outside as something added on to the mutual love of the spouses, but springs from the very heart of that mutual giving, as its fruit and fulfilment."[30] Love by its nature refuses to close in on itself: it is open to a fruitfulness that draws it beyond itself. Hence, conjugal love between a man and a woman and the transmission of life are ordered to each other. Thus the Creator has made man and woman share in the work of creation and, at same time, made them the instruments of his love, entrusting to them the responsibility for the future of humankind, through the transmission of human life.

III. LOVE IN MARRIAGE

1. A whole chapter (Four) is devoted to a discussion of love in marriage. In the first part of chapter four, Pope Francis reflects on Saint Paul's hymn to love in 1 Corinthians chapter 13. I shall now summarise a few of his reflections.

Love is patient

'Patient' here does not mean "enduring all things" because that idea is expressed in verse 7. The same word is used of God (Ex 34:6: Num 14:18) and then it means "slow to anger". It refers to the quality of a person who does not act on impulse. As the Pope explains:

> Patience takes root when I recognize that other people also have a right to live in this world, just as they are. It does not matter if they hold me back, if they unsettle my plans, or annoy me by the way they act or think, or if they are not everything I want them to be. Love always has an aspect of deep compassion that leads to accepting the other person as part of this world, even when he or she acts differently than I would like.[31]

Love is not jealous

This means that a loving person is quite happy that others succeed in life and find happiness. As the Pope points out: "True love values the other person's achievements. It does not see him or her as a threat. It frees us from the sour taste of envy. It recognizes that everyone has different gifts and a unique path in life. So it strives to discover its own road to happiness, while allowing others to find theirs."[32]

Love is generous

Real love is concerned about giving rather than getting. Saint Thomas Aquinas explains that

> it is more proper to charity to desire to love than to desire to be loved; "indeed," "mothers, who are those who love the most, seek to love more than to be loved". Consequently, love can transcend and overflow the demands of justice, "expecting nothing in return" (Luke 6:35), and the greatest of loves can lead to laying down one's life for another (cf. Jn 15:13).[33]

Love rejoices with others

It is a great thing if a person can rejoice in the talents, successes and achievements of others. It is also praiseworthy when he/she can feel happiness at the good fortune of others. As the Pope points out:

> When a loving person can do good for others, or sees that others are happy, they themselves live happily and in this way give glory to God, for "God loves a cheerful giver" (2cor 9:7). Our Lord especially appreciates those who find joy in the happiness of others. If we fail to learn how to rejoice in the well-being of others, and focus primarily on our own needs, we condemn ourselves to a joyless existence, for, as Jesus said, "it is more blessed to give than to receive" (Acts 20:35). The family must always be a place where, when something good happens to one of its members, they know that others will be there to celebrate it with them.[34]

Love bears all things

This has to do with the use of the tongue. It means "holding one's peace, even when we notice what is wrong with another person. It demands that we check our natural tendency to condemn others." Judge not, and you will not be judged (Luke 6:37). Scripture says:"Do not speak evil against one another, brothers and sisters" (Jas 4:11). As the Pope remarks:

> Married couples joined by love speak well of each other; they try to show their spouse's good side, not their weaknesses and faults. In any event, they keep silent rather than speak ill of them. This is not merely a way of acting in front of others; it springs from an interior

> attitude. Far from ingenuously claiming not to see the problems and weaknesses others, it sees those weaknesses and faults in a wider context. It recognizes that these failings are part of a bigger picture. We have to realize that all of us are a complex mixture of light and shadows. The other person is much more than the sum of the little things that annoy me.[35]

Love endures all things

This means that love has a positive attitude to everything, including every trial. This "endurance" involves not merely the ability to put up with some suffering, but also the reediness to face any challenge. "It is a love that never gives up". As the Pope reminds us:

> In family life, we need to cultivate that strength of love which can help us fight every evil threatening it. Love does not yield to resentment, scorn for others or the desire to hurt or to gain some advantage. The Christian ideal, especially in families, is a love that never gives up. I am sometimes amazed to see men or women who have had to separate from their spouse for their own protection, yet, because of their enduring conjugal love, still try to help them, even by enlisting others, in their moments of illness, suffering or trial. Here too we see a love that never gives up.[36]

Growing in Conjugal Love

Conjugal love is the love between a husband and a wife. This is a love "sanctified, enriched and illuminated by the grace of the sacrament of marriage". It combines the warmth of friendship and erotic passion. It is a gift of the Spirit. As Pope John Paul II points out: "The Spirit which the Lord pours forth gives a new heart and renders man and woman capable of loving one another as Christ loved us. Conjugal love reaches that fullness to which it is interiorly ordered: conjugal charity."[37]

According to St. Thomas Aquinas, among humans conjugal love is the greatest form of friendship: "it possesses all the traits of good friendship: concern for the good of the other, reciprocity, intimacy, warmth, stability and the remembrance born of shared life. Marriage joins to all this an indissoluble exclusivity expressed in the stable commitment to share and shape together the whole of life".[38] It is in the nature of human love that it is lasting. Lovers believe that their love is forever. Those who witness a wedding think that the union is not temporary. Children wish not only that their parents love each other but they are faithful to each other for ever. Here the Pope quotes prophet Malachi: "The Lord was witness to the covenant between you and the wife of your youth, to whom you have been faithless, though she is your companion and your wife by covenant.... Let no one be faithless to the wife of his youth. For I hate divorce, says the Lord" (Mal 2:141-16).

Quoting Vatican II, the Pope says that "marriage was not instituted solely for the procreation of children", but also that mutual love "might be properly expressed, that it should grow and mature."[39] The loving union between husband and wife is exclusive, faithful to each other and open to new life. It shares everything in constant and mutual respect.

Beauty which is different from physical or psychological appeal "enables us to appreciate the sacredness of a person, without feeling the need to possess it. In a consumerist society, the sense of beauty is impoverished and so joy fades". In such a society everything can be bought. Real love is different. As the Pope points out: "Loving another person involves the joy of contemplating and appreciating their innate beauty and sacredness, which is greater than my need. This enables me to seek their good even when they cannot belong to me, or when they are no longer physically appealing but intrusive and annoying.[40]

Pope Francis encourages young people who love each to get married, for marriage is an institution that enables their love to grow. As the Pope explains: "To opt for marriage in this way expresses a genuine and firm decision to join paths, come what may. Given its seriousness, this public commitment of love cannot be the fruit of a hasty decision, but neither can it be postponed indefinitely. Committing myself exclusively and definitively to another person always involves a risk and a bold gamble. Unwillingness to make such a commitment is selfish, calculating and petty."[41]

We should not have unrealistic expectations. Marriage and the family cannot be perfect right from the beginning. Marital love needs time and effort to grow. As Pope Francis observes: "It is much healthier to be realistic about our limits, defects and imperfections, and to respond to the call to grow together, to bring love to maturity and to strengthen the union, come what may."[42]

Dialogue is necessary for experiencing and fostering love in marriage and family "but only through long practice do we learn to dialogue well". As Pope has remarked:

> Men and women, young people and adults, communicate differently. They speak different languages and they act in different ways. Our way of asking and responding to questions, the tone we use, our timing and any number of other factors condition how well we communicate. We need to develop certain attitudes that express love and encourage authentic dialogue.[43]

Vatican II teaches that this conjugal love "embraces the good of the whole person; it can enrich the sentiments of the spirit and their physical expression with a unique dignity and ennoble them as the special features and manifestations of the friendship proper to marriage". It is such a love that can symbolize the union of the human heart with God. Here the Pope quotes the perceptive comment of A. Sertillanges; "All the mystics have affirmed that supernatural love and heavenly love find the symbols which they seek in martial love, rather than in friendship, filial devotion or devotion to a cause. And the reason is to be found precisely in its totality."[44]

Just as Jesus, as a true man, experienced and expressed his feelings so too married couples should feel free to experience and show a variety of feelings. As Pope Francis points out: "Desires, feelings, emotions, what the ancients called "the passions", all have an important place in married life". However, married people have to make sure that their entire emotional life "benefits the family as a whole and stands at the service of its common good".[45] According to the Pope: "A family is mature when the emotional life of its members becomes a form of sensitivity that neither stifles nor obscures great decisions and values, but rather follows each one's freedom, springs from it, enriches, perfects and harmonizes it in the service of all."[46]

Here Pope Francis discusses the erotic dimension of love. He points out that sexuality is God's gift to his creatures. It is necessary that sexuality be cultivated and directed in order to prevent the "impoverishment of an authentic value". Pope John Paul II has rejected the claim that the Church's teaching is a "negation of the value of human sexuality or that the Church simply tolerates sexuality because it is necessary for procreation."

One should not look down on sexual desire and "there can be no attempt whatsoever to call into question its necessity."[47] Sexual desires and passions need training. Some people fear that such a training will go against the spontaneity of sexual love. To them John Paul II replies that human persons are called to full and mature spontaneity in their relationships," a maturity that "is the gradual fruit of discernment of the impulses of one's heart."[48] This calls for discipline and self-mastery, since every human person must learn, with perseverance and consistency, the meaning of his or her body. As Pope Francis points out, "sexuality is not a means of gratification or entertainment; it is an interpersonal language wherein the other is taken seriously in his or her sacred and inviolable dignity" Besides, a healthy sexual desire, albeit closely joined to a pursuit of pleasure, always involves a sense of wonder and for that very reason can humanize the impulses. "In no way, then, can we consider the erotic dimension of love simply as a permissible evil or a burden to be tolerated for the good of the family. Rather, it must be seen as gift from God that enriches the relationship of the spouses. As a passion sublimated by a love respectful of the dignity of the other, it becomes a "pure, unadulterated affirmation" revealing the marvels of which the human heart is capable. In this way, even momentarily, we can feel that "life has turned out good and happy."[49]

Pope Francis calls attention to the danger of violence and manipulation in the exercise of sex. In his own words:

> It is, after all, a fact that sex often becomes depersonalized and unhealthy; as a result, it becomes the occasion and instrument for self-assertion and the selfish satisfaction of personal desires and instincts. In our own day, sexuality risks being poisoned by the mentality of "use and discard". The body of the other is often viewed as an object to be used as long as it offers satisfaction, and rejected once it is no longer appealing. Can we really ignore or overlook the continuing forms of domination, arrogance, abuse, sexual perversion and violence that are the product of a wrapped understanding of sexuality? Or the fact that the dignity of others and our human vocation to love thus end up being less important than an obscure need to "find oneself"?[50]

There is a lengthy discussion, in the Exhortation, of marriage and virginity. Briefly we can say that both are ways of life, but one is not better than or superior to the other. As Pope Francis wisely observes:

> The value of virginity lies in its symbolizing a love that has no need to possess the other, in this way it reflects the freedom of the Kingdom of Heaven. Virginity encourages married couples to live their own conjugal love against the backdrop of Christ's definitive love, journeying together towards the fullness of the Kingdom. For its part, conjugal love symbolizes other values. On the one hand, it is a particular reflection of that full unity in distinction found in the Trinity. The family is also a sign of Christ. It manifests the closeness of God who is a part of every human life, since he became one with us through his incarnation, death and resurrection. Each spouse becomes "one flesh" with the other as a sign of the willingness to share everything with him or her until death. Whereas virginity is an "eschatological" sign of the risen Christ, marriage is a "historical" sign for us living in this world, a sign of the earthly Christ who chose to become one with us and gave himself up for us even to shedding his blood.[51]

IV. Begetting and Educating Children

The Exhortation has two chapters on children: one titled: "Love Made Fruitful," and another: "Towards a Better Education of Children". I shall discuss them together.

1. Pope Francis opens the chapter on the begetting of children with the statement: "Love always gives life."[52] Then he quotes the meaningful words of Pope John Paul II: "Conjugal love "does not end with the couple… The couple, in giving themselves to one another, give not just themselves but also the reality of children, who are a living reflection of their love, a permanent sign of their conjugal unity and a living and inseparable synthesis of their being a father and a mother."[53]

Family is the place where a new life is welcomed as a gift of God. Each new life "allows us to appreciate the utterly gratuitous dimension of love... It is the beauty of being loved first: children are loved even before they arrive."[54] Unfortunately, "from the first moments of their lives, many children are rejected, abandoned and robbed of their childhood and future." Here, Pope sees a contradiction between the solemn declaration on human rights and the rights of children and then punishing children for the errors of adults. He believes that "when speaking of children who come into the world, no sacrifice made by adults will be considered too costly or too great, if it means the child never has to feel that he or she is a mistake or worthless or abandoned to the four winds and the arrogance of man."[55]

It is important for parents to realize that the begetting and rearing of children have implications not only for our life here on earth, but also for life hereafter. As the Pope states:

> The gift of a new child, entrusted by God to a father and mother, begins with acceptance, continues with lifelong protection and has as its final goal the joy of eternal life. By serenely contemplating the ultimate fulfilment of each human person, parents will be even more aware of the precious gift entrusted to them. For God allows parents to choose the name by which he himself will call their child for all eternity.[56]

Traditionally, the Church felt quite happy with large families which are an expression of the fruitfulness of love. As Pope John Paul II rightly observed: Responsible parenthood does not mean "unlimited procreation or lack of awareness of what is involved in rearing children, but rather the empowerment of couples to use their inviolable liberty wisely and responsibly, taking into account social and demographic realities, as well as their own situation and legitimate desires."[57]

Each child has a place in the heart of God from all eternity; when he or she is conceived God's eternal dream comes true. A pregnant woman is able to participate in God's plan by dreaming of her child.

Pope Francis urges all mothers to keep happy and let nothing rob them of their happiness. These mothers must take care that no fears, worries or other people's comments or problems lessen their joy at being God's means of bringing a new life to the world. They can join in Mary's song of joy: "My soul proclaims the greatness of the Lord". They should ask God to preserve their joy.

Children, once born, need to receive the spiritual gift of love along with nourishment and care. They should be helped to become aware with certainty that they are loved. "This love is shown to them through the gift of their personal name, the sharing of the language, looks of love and the brightness of a smile. In this way they learn that the beauty of human relationships touches our soul, seeks our freedom, accepts the difference of others, recognizes and respects them as a partner in dialogue."[58]

For the child's integral and harmonious development he/she has to receive love from both the parents. Each of the spouses "contributes in a distinct way to the upbringing of a child. Respecting the child's dignity means affirming his or her natural right to have a father and a mother. Together they manifest the maternal and paternal face of the Lord."[59] Together they teach the value of reciprocity, of respect for differences and of being able to give and take.

Married couple, precisely because of their experience of the power of love, have to reach out to the less fortunate people around them. They should have a clear awareness of their social obligations. They are called to bind the wounds of the outcast, to foster a culture of encounter and to fight for justice.

It is important for nuclear families not to isolate themselves. They have to interact with the wider family made up of parents, uncles, aunts, cousins and even immediate neighbours. There is need to take good care of the elderly. "We must reawaken the collective sense of gratitude, of appreciation, of hospitality which makes the elderly feel like a living part of the family/community". Besides, the elderly help us to appreciate the continuity of the generations by their charism of bridging the gap. "Many people can testify that they owe their initiation into the Christian life to their grandparents." As Pope Francis remarks: "Their words, their affection or simply their presence help children to realize that history did not begin with them, that they are now part of an age-old pilgrimage and that they need to respect all that came before them. A society will move forward if it respects the wisdom of the elderly."[60]

The relationship between brothers and sisters in the family has implications not only for themselves but also for society at large. It is in the family that we learn to live together as one. The family introduces fraternity into the world. The initial experience of fraternity in the family, nourished by love and acceptance, enables young people to foster brotherly, sisterly relationships in society. As the Pope remarks: "Growing up with brothers and sisters makes for a beautiful experience of caring for and helping one another. For fraternity in families is especially radiant when we see the care, the patience, the affection that surround the little brother or sister who is frail, sick or disabled". It must be acknowledged that having a brother or a sister who loves you is a profound, precious and unique experience. "Children do need to be patiently taught to treat one another as brothers and sisters".[61]

The Education of Children

In this Apostolic Exhortation there is a chapter devoted to "A Better Education of Children". In this chapter the Pope discusses some important areas of the education of children.

At the beginning the Pope makes two observations which are quite significant:

1. It is important for parents to keep track of where their children are. They have to be "concerned about who is providing them with entertainment, who is entering their rooms through television and electronic devices, and with whom they are spending their free time". If parents are excessively concerned about knowing where their children are and controlling all their movements they will only seek to dominate space. "But this is no way to educate, strengthen and prepare their children to face challenges. What is most important is the ability lovingly to help them grow in freedom, maturity, overall discipline and real autonomy. Only in this way will children come to possess the wherewithal needed to fend for themselves and to act intelligently and prudently whenever they meet with difficulties."[62]
2. The real question is not where our children are physically, or with whom they are at a given time, "but rather where they are existentially, where they stand in terms of their convictions, goals, desires and dreams". Here the Pope poses some questions to the parents: "Do we seek to understand 'where' they really are in their journey? Where is their 'soul', do we really know? Above all, do we want to know?"[63]

Ethical Formation

Generally speaking, parents can rely on schools to impart basic instruction to children. But they cannot leave the moral formation of their children to others. As the Pope observes:

> A person's affective and ethical development is ultimately grounded in a particular experience, namely, that his or her parents can be trusted. This means that parents, as educators, are responsible, by their affection and example, for instilling in their children trust and loving respect.[64]

Shaping the will of their children, fostering good habits and a natural inclination to goodness are also the responsibility of the parents.

Parents have to be consistent in their own moral actions. It often happens that our conscience points to a clear moral decision but we are often influenced by other factors which prove to be more attractive and more powerful. This is an area where parents have to become more consistent. They have to realize that what the intellect sees as good is good for us here and now. They have to act accordingly. "A good ethical education includes showing a person that it is in his own interest to do what is right. Today, it is less and less effective to demand something that calls for effort and sacrifice without clearly pointing to the benefits which it can bring."[65]

In this context it must be pointed out that correction can be an incentive to good behaviour and personal growth. Children who are lovingly corrected come to realize that their parents love and care for them. A child who does wrong has to be corrected, but not treated as an enemy. Parents need to understand that some kind of misbehavior flows from the frailty and limitations typical of youth. A constant attitude of punishing children would lead to discouragement and resentment.[66]

It is important for parents to reflect on how to ensure that discipline does not discourage children but serves as a stimulus to moral growth. In the question of discipline parents have to avoid two extremes. One would be to yield to the child's desires all the time. Such a child will grow up with a sense of his/her rights, but not his/her responsibilities. The other would be to deprive children of an awareness of their dignity, personal identity and their rights. Such children will grow up fully aware of their responsibilities, and a need to behave according to the wishes of other people.

It is in the family, which is the first school of human values, that we learn to use freedom wisely. "Certain inclinations develop in childhood and become so deeply rooted that they remain throughout life either as an attraction to a particular value or a natural repugnance to certain ways of acting."[67]

Children have to be helped to realize that instant gratification of all their desires is not possible. We have to wait for certain things. Children need to learn self-mastery and detachment from their impulses. "When children realize that they have to be responsible for themselves, their self-esteem is enriched. This in turn teaches them to respect the freedom of others."[68]

It is in the family that children are socialized. There they learn how to relate to others, to share and listen, to be patient and show respect, to help one another and live as one. They also have to understand that the world and society are our home. They have to learn how to live in that greater home. They have to be taught how to care for the environment which is our common home. "The family is the principal agent of an integral ecology because it is the primary social subject which contains within it the two fundamental principles of human civilization- the principle of communion and the principle of fruitfulness". "It is necessary that children are helped to be sensitive to human illness. Times of illness enable family bonds to grow stronger.[69]

Children have to learn how to use the media in a critical and creative way. Parents cannot ignore the risks that these new forms of communication pose for children and adolescents.[70]

Sex Education: Vatican Council spoke of the need for "a positive and prudent sex education" to be imparted to children and adolescents "as they grow older", with "due weight being given to the advances in the psychological, pedagogical and didactic sciences". It is doubtful if our educational institutions have taken up this challenge."[71]

Sex education should be looked at within the broader framework of an education for love, for mutual self-giving. As the Pope points out:Sex education should also include respect and appreciation for differences, as a way of helping the young to overcome their self-absorption and to be open and accepting of others. Beyond the understandable difficulties which individuals may experience, the young need to be helped to accept their own body as it was created, for "thinking that we enjoy absolute power over our own bodies turns, often subtly, into thinking that we enjoy absolute power over creation.[72]

V. Pastoral Perspectives and Pastoral Practices

Chapter six of *Amoris Laetitia* discusses some pastoral perspectives. And chapter eight deals with some pastoral practices. I shall discuss both of them in this section. To begin with, the pastoral perspectives. As the Pope points out: The Synod Fathers emphasized that Christian families, by the grace of the sacrament of matrimony, are the principal agents of the family apostolate, above all through "their joy-filled witness as domestic churches."[73]

The Church has to denounce cultural, social, political and economic factors "that prevent authentic family life and lead to discrimination, poverty, exclusion and violence".

1. The parish has to take the main responsibility for the pastoral care of families. To do this effectively there is the need for a "more adequate formation... of priests, deacons, men and women religious, catechists and other pastoral workers". From "the worldwide consultation it became clear that ordained ministers often lack the training needed to deal with the complex problems currently facing families." Hence, "seminarians should receive more extensive, interdisciplinary, and not merely doctrinal, formation in the areas of engagement and marriage... It is helpful for seminarians to combine time in the seminary with time spent in the parishes. There they can have greater contact with concrete realities of family life..."[74]

The Church also needs to train lay leaders who can be a great help in the pastoral care of the families. Here we can enlist the collaboration of teachers, community leaders, physicians, advocates and social workers. People competent in psychology, sociology and marital counselling can be asked to make a contribution to the training of lay leaders.

Besides, as Pope Francis observes, "Professionals, especially those with practical experience, help keep pastoral initiatives grounded in the real situations and concrete concerns of families."[75]

2. The Church needs to take concrete steps to prepare engaged couples for marriage. As the Pope reported:

The Synod Fathers stated in a number of ways that we need to help young people discover the dignity and beauty of marriage. They should be helped to perceive the attraction of a complete union that elevates and perfects the social dimension of existence, gives sexuality its deepest meaning, and benefits children by offering them the best context for their growth and development.[76]

Marriage preparation has to help the couple to realize that the wedding ceremony is not the end but a new beginning – a commitment to work together to improve the quality of their marriage. They have to undertake a common journey in which they should face all trials and difficulties together so that their love for each other grows and their marriage matures.

Besides, "the couple should be encouraged to make the liturgical celebration a profound experience and to appreciate the meaning of each of its signs". They are the ministers of the sacrament of matrimony and the commitment they make to each other through the words of consent is a sign of Christ's relationship with the Church. They should be helped to become "aware that in the conjugal pact there is expressed and realized the mystery that has its origin in God himself".

The couple has to helped to realize that marriage is not something that happens once for all. As the Pope observes:

> Their union is real and irrevocable, confirmed and consecrated by the sacrament of matrimony. Yet joining their lives, the spouses assume an active and creative role in a lifelong project. Their gaze now has to be directed to the future that, with the help of God's grace, they are daily called to build. For this very reason, neither spouse can expect the other to be perfect. Each must set aside all illusions and accept the other as he or she actually is: an unfinished product, needing to grow, a work in progress. A persistently critical attitude towards one's partner is a sign that marriage was not entered into as a project to be worked on together, with patience, understanding, tolerance and generosity.

Marriage and conjugal love mature slowly.[77] The pastoral care of newly married couples must also involve encouraging them to be generous in bestowing life. "In accord with the personal and fully human character of conjugal love, family planning fittingly takes place as the result a consensual dialogue between the spouses, respect for times and consideration of the dignity of the partner. In this sense, the teaching of the Encyclical *Humanae Vitae* and the Apostolic Exhortation *Familiaris Consortio* ought to be taken up anew in order to counter a mentality that is often hostile to life... Decisions involving responsible parenthood presupposes the formation of conscience, which is 'the most secret core and sanctuary of a person. There each one is alone with God, whose voice echoes in the depths of the heart' (*Gaudium et Spes*, 16). The more the couple tries to listen in conscience to God and his commandments (cf. Rom 2:15), and is accompanied spiritually, the more their decision will be profoundly free of subjective caprice and accommodation to prevailing social more.

3. It is important for couples to learn how to forgive and how to accept forgiveness. Some families break up when spouses engage in mutual recrimination, but "experience shows that with proper assistance and acts of reconciliation, through grace, a great percentage of troubled marriages find a

solution in a satisfying manner. To know how to forgive and to feel forgiven is a basic experience in family life."[78] The arduous art of reconciliation, which requires the support of grace, needs the generous cooperation of relatives and friends, and sometimes even outside help and professional assistance.

The Pope Francis makes several suggestions for the pastoral care of persons in difficult marital situations.

1) Special discernment is also necessary when dealing with those who are divorced and remarried, who are involved in mixed marriages, who are married to non-Christians, in civil marriages, and those who are merely cohabiting.
2) The Christian community has to remember that there are many factors that diminish or nullify the imputability of an action. Here the Pope quotes the *Catechism of the Catholic Church*: "imputability and responsibility for an action can be diminished or even nullified by ignorance, inadvertence, duress, fear, habit, inordinate attachments, and other psychological or social factors."[79] In another paragraph, the Catechism refers once again to circumstances which mitigate moral responsibility, and mentions at length "affective immaturity, force of acquired habit, conditions of anxiety or other psychological or social factors that lesson or even extenuate moral culpability. For this reason, a negative judgment about an objective situation does not imply a judgment about the imputability or culpability of the person involved.[80] On the basis of these convictions, I consider very fitting what many Synod Fathers wanted to affirm: "Under certain circumstances people find it very difficult to act differently. Therefore, while upholding a general rule, it is necessary to recognize that responsibility with respect to certain actions or decisions is not the same in all cases. Pastoral discernment, while taking into account a person's properly formed conscience, must take responsibility for these situations. Even the consequences of actions taken are not necessarily the same in all cases."[81]
3) An awareness of the weight of mitigating circumstances should make the Church more sensitive and merciful: As the Pope states: At the same time, from our awareness of the weight of mitigating circumstances-psychological, historical and even biological – it follows that "without detracting from the evangelical ideal, there is a need to accompany with mercy and patience the eventual stages of personal growth as these progressively appear", making room for "the Lord's mercy, which spurs us on to do our best".

VI. The Spirituality of Marriage and the Family

Pope Francis has tried, in the last chapter of the Apostolic Exhortation, to describe the main characteristics of the spirituality of marriage and the family.

1. A Spirituality of Communion

As the Pope remarks:

> The Lord dwells in real and concrete families with all their daily troubles and struggles, joys and hopes. Living in a family makes it hard for us to feign or lie; we cannot hide behind a mask. If that authenticity is inspired by love, then the Lord reigns there, with his joy and his peace. The spirituality of family love is made up of thousands of small but real gestures. In that variety of gifts and encounters which deepen communion, God has his dwelling place. This mutual concern "brings together the human and the divine", for it is filled with the love of God. In the end, marital spirituality is a spirituality of the bond, in which divine love dwells.[82]

The brotherly/sisterly and communal demands of family life enable the couples to grow in openness of heart and thus to ever fuller encounter with Lord. St John says: "the one who hates his brother is in the darkness and walks in the darkness (1 Jn 2: 11). Such a person "abides in death" (1 Jn 3: 14) and "does not know God" (1 Jn 4: 8). As Pope Benedict XVI points out, "closing our eyes to our neighbour also blinds us to God", and love is the only light which can "constantly illuminate a world grown dim."[83] If we love one another, God abides in us and his love is perfected in us" (1 Jn 4:12). Since the human person is by nature social, and the first and the basic expression of that social dimension is the married couple and the family, spirituality becomes incarnate in the communion of the family.

2. Gathered in Prayer in the Light of Easter

If a family is centred on Christ he will unify and illumine its entire life. Times of pain and difficulty will be experienced in union with God's cross. In the darkest hours of family's life, union with Christ in his abandonment can help to avoid a breakup. Besides, moments of joy, relaxation, celebration and even sexuality can be experienced as a share in the life of the Risen Lord.[84]

Family prayer is a way of expressing and strengthening the paschal faith. Everyday some time should be set apart for family prayer-for thanking God for all his blessings and for asking for his help, protection, and guidance in its life. Common participation in the Eucharist can be a source of peace and joy. "For the food of the Eucharist offers the spouses the strength and the incentive to live the marriage covenant as a domestic Church."[85]

3. A Spirituality of Exclusive and Free Love

As Pope Francis observes: "Marriage is also the experience of belonging completely to another person. Spouses accept the challenge and aspiration of supporting one another, growing old together, and in this way reflecting God's own faithfulness. This firm decision, which shapes a style of life, is an "interior requirement of the covenant of conjugal love", since "a person who cannot choose to love for ever can hardly love for even a single day."[86]

Day in and day out the spouses have to make an effort to grow in conjugal love. "In this way, each spouse is for the other a sign and instrument of the closeness of the Lord".

In course of time, the couple's love attains the height of freedom and this becomes the basis of a healthy autonomy. This occurs when each of the spouses realizes that the other is not his/her own, but has an absolute Master, the Lord. "No one but God can presume to take over the deepest and the most personal core of the loved one; he alone can be the ultimate centre of their life... The space which each of the spouses makes for their personal relationship with God not only helps to heal the hurts of life in common, but also enables the spouses to find in the love of God the deepest source of meaning in their lives."[87]

4. A Spirituality of care, concern and an incentive

According to the Pope : "Christian couples are, for each other, for their children and for their relatives, cooperators of grace and witnesses of the faith". God calls them to bestow life and to care for life. For this reason the family "has always been the nearest 'hospital'". So let us care for one another, guide and encourage one another, and experience this as part of our family spirituality.[88]

Each of those who live with us has to be given full attention since he/she possesses infinite dignity as a person loved by God. This conviction can help us to be tender in our love for them

As this Exhortation has often noted: "No family drops down perfectly formed; families need constantly to grow and mature in the ability to love. This is a never-ending vocation born of the full communion of the Trinity, the profound unity between Christ and his Church, the loving community which is the Holy Family of Nazareth, and the pure fraternity existing among the saints of heaven."[89]

The Exhortation concludes with a prayer to the Holy family asking it "to make us once more mindful of the sacredness and inviolability of the family and its beauty in God's plan".

VII. Reflections

This is a rich document which deals with the different dimensions of marriage and the family today. It incorporates into it the findings of two Synods of Bishops on marriage and family held in Rome in 2014 and 2016. As Pope Francis has written in the Introduction. I must also say that the Synod process proved both impressive and illuminating. I am grateful for the many contributions that helped me to appreciate more fully the problems faced by families throughout the world. The various interventions of the Synod Fathers, to which I paid close heed, made up, as it were, a multifaceted gem reflecting many legitimate concerns and honest questions.

1. The Pope takes care to incorporate into this Exhortation the teachings of Popes Paul VI, John Paul II and Benedict XVI. Hence, there is a clear continuity in the Church's understanding of marriage and the family.
2. There is in this document an insightful discussion of conjugal love. The longest chapter in the document is devoted to it.
3. Pope Francis pleads for a sympathetic understanding of people caught up in difficult marital situations. He suggests that the Church adopt a compassionate pastoral approach to them. He points out that because of a variety of mitigating circumstances these people may not be subjectively as guilty as it appears on the surface. Besides, the Church is called to bear witness to Christ's mercy in all situations.
4. What the Pope has to say about the begetting and education of Children is quite helpful to married people and their families.
5. To me this Exhortation appears to be quite long – 68000 words and a bit verbose. In this day and age people may not have the patience to read such a lengthy document. But if they do read it carefully, they will profit a lot since this is an inspiring Exhortation.

Notes

1. *Amoris Laetitia* (AL) n. 4
2. *AL* n. 1
3. *Ibid.*
4. *AL* n. 7
5. As quoted in *AL* n. 32
6. *AL* n. 38
7. *AL* 33
8. *Ibid.*
9. *Ibid.*
10. *Ibid.*
11. *AL* 43
12. *AL* 35
13. *AL* 36
14. *AL* 37
15. *Ibid.*
16. *AL* 43
17. *AL* 42
18. *AL* 48
19. *AL* 51
20. *Ibid.*
21. *AL* 11
22. *AL* 12
23. *AL* 15
24. *AL* 62
25. As quoted in *AL* 66
26. *AL* 67
27. As quote in *AL* 68

28. *AL* 72
29. *AL* 74
30. As quoted in *AL* 80
31. *AL* 92
32. *AL* 95
33. *AL* 102
34. *AL* 110
35. *AL* 113
36. *AL* 119
37. *AL* 120
38. As quoted in *AL* 123
39. As quoted in *AL* 125
40. *AL* 127
41. *AL* 132
42. *AL* 135
43. *AL* 136
44. As quoted in *AL* 142
45. *AL* 146
46. *Ibid.*
47. *AL* 150
48. As quoted in *AL* 151
49. *AL* 152
50. *AL* 153
51. *AL* 161
52. *AL* 165
63. *Ibid.*
54. *AL* 166
55. *Ibid.*
56. *Ibid.*
57. As quoted in *AL* 167
58. *AL* 172
59. *Ibid.*
60. *AL* 192
61. *AL* 195
62. *AL* 261
63. *Ibid.*
64. *AL* 263
65. *AL* 265
66. *AL* 269
67. *AL* 274
68. *AL* 276
69. *AL* 277
70. *AL* 278
71. *AL* 280
72. *AL* 285
73. *AL* 200
74. *AL* 203
75. *AL* 204
76. *AL* 213
77. *AL* 218

78. *AL* 236
79. As quoted in *AL* 302
80. *Ibid.*
81. *Ibid.*
82. *AL* 315
83. As quoted in *AL* 316
84. *AL* 317
85. *AL* 318
86. *AL* 319
87. *AL* 320
88. *AL* 321
89. *AL* 325

16

THE FORMATION OF PRIESTS TODAY

A Study of "The Gift of Priestly Vocation"

A recent Roman document titled: "The Gift of Priestly Vocation" spells out new guidelines for priestly formation. It was issued by the Congregation for the Clergy on December 8, 2016. It is a thoroughly revised plan for priestly formation which was first issued in 1970 and then revised in 1980. Because of the rapid changes in "historical, socio-cultural and ecclesiastical contexts, the guidelines needed to be revamped, renewed and restored to the centre," said Cardinal Beniamino Stella, Prefect of the Congregation for the Clergy.[1] He added that "inspiration was drawn from Pope Francis' teaching and spirituality, especially regarding temptations tied to money, to authoritarian exercise of power, to rigid legalism and to vainglory."[2] He is of the view that "in the life of the Church innovations are never separate from tradition, but, on the contrary, integrate it and enhance it."[3] The Cardinal also pointed out that the document was greatly influenced by Pope John Paul II's *Pastores Dabo Vobis*, published in 1992, which seeks to promote an "integral formation," that is, "the ability to unite, in a balanced way, the human as well as the spiritual, intellectual and pastoral dimensions, through a gradual instructional personalised course."[4]

1. There are two remarkable things about the document

1) It is the fruit of wide consultation.[5] A preliminary draft was produced in the spring of 2014. It was then discussed in the Plenary Assembly of the Congregation for the Clergy. The Cardinal and Bishop members and the invited experts offered proposals and suggestions for the improvement of the draft. In the light of these proposals and suggestions a fuller text was drawn up and sent to different dicasteries of the Roman Curia asking for

their comments and suggestions. "During 2015 the text was also sent to numerous Conferences of Bishops and Apostolic Nunciatures in order to seek their opinion and broaden the scope of consultation and reflection." This was done in a spirit of synodality, that is so frequently highlighted by Pope Francis.

The Congregation for the Clergy held an international Conference on 19-20 November 2015 during which Cardinals, Bishops, professors, formators and experts made many valuable suggestions for the revision of the text on priestly formation.

"At the end of this process of consultation and in the light of the suggestions received, a definitive text was drafted and was placed before Pope Francis for his approval.

2) The Document shows great sensitivity to the enormous socio-cultural diversity in the world. That is why it is asking the Bishops' Conference of every country to draw up a National Programme of Priestly Formation taking seriously into account the socio-cultural situation there as well as the guidelines spelt out in this document.[6] While safeguarding the authority of the diocesan bishop, the National Programme, prepared by the Bishops' Conferences, seeks to harmonise priestly formation across the country, in this way facilitating a dialogue between Bishops and formators, which will benefit both the seminarians and the seminaries. The National Programme should always include the following elements.[7]
   - At least a summary description of the particular social, cultural and ecclesial context, in which the future priests will find themselves exercising their ministry;
   - A summary of any agreements that may have been reached by the Conference of Bishops concerning the organisation of Seminaries in its country;
   - Some reference to the pastoral care of vocations and the means available;
   - A description of the stages of formation, placed in the context of the particular situation of the country;
   - A description of the means to be adopted to provide for the dimensions of formation (human, spiritual, intellectual and pastoral).
   - The programme of propaedeutic, philosophical and theological studies, including a presentation of the subjects, with some indication of the objectives and contents of each, along with the number of credits required for each discipline.

2. Priestly Vocation

Among the many vocations which the Holy Spirit calls forth in the People of God, the vocation to the ministerial priesthood calls one to "participate in the hierarchical priesthood of Christ."[8] As John Paul II teaches, it is the mission of the

Church "to care for the birth, discernment and fostering of vocations, particularly those to the priesthood."[9] Hence, vocation promotion is an important ministry of the Church, especially the local church. Bishops, priests and the laity, particularly parents and teachers, have to cooperate in this activity. Remembering that the Christ has asked us to pray to the Lord of the harvest to send labourers into his harvest, the entire people of God should seriously and unceasingly pray for vocations, especially those to the priesthood.

The document asks the diocesan authorities to pay special attention to two types of vocations. "Today, given the growth in mature vocations among those with one or more work experiences, there is a growing awareness of the need to give particular attention to this age group."[10] Further, the document cites the words of Pope John Paul II: "Special attention needs to be given to vocations among indigenous peoples. They need a formation which takes account of their culture."[11] In the Indian context something similar can be said of vocations among scheduled castes and scheduled tribes.

3. Priestly Identity

In order that the formation imparted in our Major Seminaries may be effective, we need to have a clear idea of the identity of the priesthood. Vatican II reminds us that the nature and mission of priests must be understood within the Church, the People of God. The entire People of God participates in the saving work of Christ and are in fact a priestly people. The ministerial priesthood is to be understood as a service to the glory of God and to the brothers and sisters in their baptismal priesthood.[12] In communion with the order of Bishops, priests are inseparably part of the ecclesial community and, at the same time, by the will of Christ and in continuance of the work of the Apostles, have been constituted pastors and leaders in the Church.

As the document points out, "the priest is called to cultivate missionary zeal, exercising his pastoral responsibility with humility as an authoritative leader, teacher of the word and minister of the sacraments, practising his spiritual fatherhood fruitfully.[13] As Pope Francis clearly states: "Every authority is exercised in a spirit of service, as '*amoris officium*' (office of love) and unpretentious dedication for the good of the flock."[14]

The priestly vocation begins with the gift of God's grace. This gift is expressed through the mediation of the Church which calls and sends a person to engage in the priestly ministry. The personal response develops through a process, which begins with an awareness of the gift received, and matures gradually with the help of priestly spirituality, until it becomes a stable way of life, with its obligations and rights, and a specific mission accepted by the one who is ordained.[15]

In the introduction the document makes two important assertions:

1) The journey of priestly formation has four characteristic elements: "one, integral, grounded in community and missionary in spirit.[16] Formation

must be seen through a unifying lens, which takes into account the four dimensions of formation – human, spiritual, intellectual and pastoral. The entire journey of formation must never be reduced to a single aspect to the detriment of others, but it must always be an integrated journey of the disciple called to the priesthood. The formation of priests has an eminently communitarian character. Vocation to the priesthood is a gift that God gives to the Church and to the world. Such a vocation is discovered and accepted within a community. And formation to the priesthood takes place in the Seminary in the context of an educating community. This community enables the seminarian to become part of the family of the presbyterate, at the service a particular community. In order to be effective in their ministry, priest formators "must consider themselves to be a formative community, sharing a common responsibility, with regard 'to the duties entrusted to each one." Finally, formation is clearly missionary in character since its goal is participation in the mission of evangelization entrusted by Christ to the Church. Hence, Seminarians have to become missionary disciples, who are in love with the Master, shepherds with the "smell of the sheep," who live in their midst to bring the mercy of God to them.

2) Within this single integrated formation, two phases can be identified: the initial and the ongoing.[17] The "initial" formation is divided into various stages: the propaedeutic stage; the study of philosophy or the discipleship stage; the study of theology or the configurative stage, and pastoral stage or that of vocational integration stage.

The **Propaedeutic** Stage

The propaedeutic stage is a preparatory stage which is thought to be necessary because of the experience of recent decades. It should last no less than one year and no more than two years. Its principal objective is to provide a solid basis for the spiritual life of the candidate and to nurture greater self-awareness for his personal growth. It is a time to become personally convinced of one's vocation to the priesthood.[18]

4. Study of Philosophy and Theology

It is quite significant that the formation imparted in the Major Seminaries is conceived in deeply spiritual terms. The first two years during which the seminarian will study philosophy is called the discipleship stage. The disciple is one whom the Lord has called "to stay with him" (See Mk 3:14), to follow him and to become a missionary of the Gospel. Each day he will learn to enter into the secrets of the Kingdom of God. Staying with Jesus becomes a spiritual journey that transforms the life of the seminarian. The dynamic discipleship which lasts for the whole of life and includes all priestly formation pedagogically requires a specific stage when all possible efforts are made to root the seminarian in the *sequela Christi*, listening to his word, keeping it in his heart and putting into practice.

The last four years of formation in the Major Seminary during which the seminarian will do theology is termed the "configuration" stage. During this stage formation concentrates on the configuration of the seminarian to Christ, Shepherd and Servant, so that united to him he can make a gift of self to others. This configuration demands that the seminarians enter profoundly into the contemplation of the person of Jesus Christ, sent by the Father, as Shepherd of the people of God. It will make the relationship with Christ more intimate and personal, and, at the same time, will lead to an awareness and acceptance of his priestly identity. This state calls for a constant responsibility in living the theological and cardinal virtues and the evangelical counsels. It demands docility to the action of God. It also seeks for a gradual recreation of one's own personal history in the light of pastoral charity, which animates, forms and motivates the life of a priest.

5. The Foundations of Formation

There is a whole chapter (III) in the document which deals with the foundations of formation. To begin with, there is the person of the seminarian. "On the one hand, he is characterised by talents and gifts that have been moulded by grace; on the other, he is marked by his limits and frailty."[19] The task of formation is to enable the seminarian to integrate these two aspects of his personality with the help of the Holy Spirit and grow into a balanced person, avoiding fragmentation, superficiality and partiality. The time of priestly formation is a period of testing, maturing and discernment by both the seminarian and his formators.

The seminarian is called to go out of himself and journey in Christ towards the Father and towards others embracing his vocation to the priesthood; he has to work with the Holy Spirit to "achieve a serene and creative interior synthesis between his strengths and weaknesses."[20] The formation process helps the seminarian to bring all dimensions of their personality to Christ, who will enable him consciously to be free for God and for others. "In fact it is only in the Crucified and Risen Christ that this path of integration finds meaning and completion." Effective pastoral care of the people demands that the priest have a solid formation and interior maturity. It is not enough for him to have the appearance of a virtuous person, who practises merely external obedience to an abstract principle. He is called to act with great inner freedom. He has to internalise, day after day, the spirit of the Gospel and to establish a deep personal friendship with Christ, leading him to imbibe his sentiments and attitudes.

By this intimate relationship with Christ and by their fraternal communion, seminarians will be helped to recognise and correct "spiritual worldliness: obsession with personal appearance, a presumed theological and spiritual certainty, narcissism and authoritarianism, the attempt to dominate others, a merely external and ostentatious preoccupation with the liturgy, vainglory, individualism, the inability to listen to others and every form of careerism." Instead they have to be formed in simplicity, sobriety, serene dialogue and authenticity. As disciples of the Master, they should learn to live and act with the pastoral charity, that flows from being "servants of Christ and stewards of the mysteries of God" (See 1 Cor 4:1).

Accompaniment is an important means of formation. Seminarians need to be accompanied in a personal way during the various stages of their formation by the formators.[21] The purpose of personal accompaniment is to carry out vocational discernment and to form the missionary disciple. For accompaniment to be effective it is necessary that the seminarian should know himself and let himself be known, relating to the formators with sincerity and transparency. A necessary element in the process of accompaniment is mutual trust.[22] The seminary should explore and describe concrete ways in which this trust can be fostered and safeguarded. Above all, those conditions should be fostered which can create a peaceful atmosphere of trust and mutual confidence: fraternity, empathy, understanding, the ability to listen and to share.

Dimensions

There is a certain freshness in the way the document deals with the four dimensions of formation – the human, the spiritual, the intellectual and the pastoral.

To begin with human formation. As the document states: "The divine call engages and involves the 'concrete' human person. Formation for the priesthood must necessarily provide adequate means to allow for maturation in view of an authentic exercise of priestly ministry. To that end, the seminarian is called upon to develop his personality, having Christ, the perfect man, as his model."[23]

A correct and harmonious spirituality demand a well-structured humanity, since grace builds on nature. It does not cancel nature, but perfects it. Hence it is necessary for the seminarian to acquire such qualities as humility, courage, common sense, magnanimity, right judgement and discretion, tolerance and transparency, love of truth and honesty.

Human formation, which is the foundation of all priestly formation, has to promote the integral growth of the person and allow the integration of all its dimensions – the physical, the psychological, the moral and the aesthetic.[24] It should foster the establishment of a stable personality, characterised by emotional balance, self-control and a well-integrated sexuality. It has to enable the seminarian to arrive gradually at a well-formed conscience. This means that he has become a responsible person able to make right decisions, gifted with right judgement and able to have an objective perception of persons and events. Such a perspective should lead the seminarian to have a balanced sense of self-respect. It is also important for him to cultivate a sense of beauty.

For an effective human formation, it is necessary that the seminarian is aware of his life history and be ready to share it with his formators.[25] This will enable them to plan their personal accompaniment in such a way that it is really helpful to the seminarian.

An unmistakable sign of the harmonious development of the personality of the seminarian is his mature capacity to relate with men and women of different ages and social conditions.[26] It is important that the formators take into consideration the relationship between the seminarian and women since it affects "the seminarian not only in the sphere of his personal life but also with a view to his future ministry."[27]

The understanding of and familiarity with the feminine are beneficial to the human growth of the seminarian. It is important that a seminarian learns from women and lets himself be influenced by the feminine genius.[23]

Through the human formation he has received the seminarian becomes capable of self-determination and living with responsibility through an awareness of his own weaknesses which are always present in his personality. From what has been said about human formation it is quite clear that only a good and mature person can be good priest and an effective pastor.

As the document makes it clear, "the spiritual formation is aimed at nourishing and sustaining communion with God and with our brothers and sisters, in friendship with Jesus, the Good Shepherd, and with an attitude of docility to the Holy Spirit."[28]

This formation should foster a personal union with Christ which is born of and sustained by prolonged and silent prayer. This union will enable the seminarian to be like Christ totally committed to the will of the Father.[29]

Besides, the liturgical year enables the seminarian to absorb its spirituality by interiorising the Scriptural texts and liturgical prayers. A seminarian should cultivate a healthy relationship to the Holy Eucharist.[30]

Regular and frequent celebration of the sacrament of reconciliation, for which the seminarian should prepare by a daily examination of conscience, becomes an occasion to recognise with humility his own sins and frailties.

Spiritual direction is a means for the integral growth of the person. The seminarian should be left free to choose his spiritual director from among those who are made available by the Seminary. A high quality of spiritual accompaniment is necessary for the effectiveness of the whole process of formation.

Finally, the seminarian should be in touch with certain expressions of popular piety and religion, especially those approved by the Magisterium. One day he, as priest, will be called upon to discern, guide and accept some of them because of their spiritual effectiveness.[31]

The intellectual formation is aimed at helping the seminarian to acquire real competence in philosophy and theology, along with a more general education which will enable the seminarian to proclaim the Gospel message to people of our day in a manner that is credible. It seeks to help them to enter into dialogue with the contemporary world[32] and to uphold the truth of faith by the light of reason, thereby revealing its beauty. Candidates for the priesthood must diligently strive to deepen their knowledge of philosophical and theological sciences, with a good introduction to canon law, social science and history. The intellectual formation seeks to give a reason for hope (See 1 Pet 3:15) and to allow Divine Revelation to become known.

Pastoral formation is vitally important. In fact, the entire priestly formation must be permeated by a pastoral spirit.[33] This will enable the seminarian to demonstrate the same compassion, generosity, love for all, especially the poor, and zeal for the Kingdom of God, that characterised the ministry of Jesus Christ. The pastoral formation should be such as to help the seminarian to acquire the inner freedom to live the apostolate as service, able to see the work of God in the hearts and lives of the people. Gradually, the seminarian will begin to see himself as a group leader and as a man of communion. He will do so by attentive listening and careful discernment of situations, as well as cooperating with others.

It is noteworthy that, according to this document, pastoral formation is not primarily meant to help the seminarian to master some pastoral skills. It is aimed at enabling the seminarian to cultivate certain attitudes and to acquire certain values that will make him an effective pastor.

There is a whole chapter (VI) devoted to the agents of formation. From a faith perspective, God, who calls the seminarian to the priesthood, is the primary agent of formation. As the document clearly states, "the principal agent of formation is the most Holy Trinity, who shapes every seminarian according to the plan of the Father, both through the presence of Christ in his word and in the brothers and sisters of the community, and through the many actions of the Holy Spirit. In the formation of a priest, the primacy of the working of the Holy Spirit calls for reciprocal listening and cooperation among all the members of the ecclesial community."[34]

The members of the diocese play a significant role in the formation of a priest – the bishop, the presbyterate, the formators in the seminary, the professors, the administrative personnel and the family and the parish community. The document adds that the presence of women in the seminarian's journey of formation has its own formative significance.[35] Their presence helps to instil a recognition of how men and women complement one another.

By way of conclusion, I wish to make two comments.

1) It is remarkable that the document looks upon formation as a journey. By repeatedly referring to the journey of formation, it makes it abundantly clear that formation is not a closed system but a dynamic process.
2) The document shows great respect for the person of the seminarian. It declares that the seminarian is a "necessary and irreplaceable agent of his own formation."[36]

By and large, this is a modern and inspiring document which spells out concrete guidelines for the formation of priests today.

Notes

1. In an interview reported in *Osservatore Romano*, 7 December, 2016
2. *Ibid*
3. *Ibid.*
4. *Ibid.*
5. Congregation for the Clergy, *The Gift of Priestly Vocation*, Rome, 2016, n. 2
6. *Ibid.* n. 3
7. *Ibid.* n. 7
8. *Ibid.* n. 11
9. *Ibid.* n. 13
10. *Ibid.* 14
11. *Ibid.* 25
12. *Ibid.* 31
13. *Ibid.* 33
14. *Ibid.* 34
15. *Ibid.*
16. *Ibid.* n. 3
17. *Ibid.*
18. *Ibid.*
19. *Ibid.* n. 28
20. *Ibid.* n. 29
21. *Ibi*d. n. 44
22. *Ibid.* n. 47
23. *Ibid.* n. 93
24. *Ibid.* n. 94
25. *Ibid.*
26. *Ibid.* n. 95
27. *Ibid.*
28. *Ibid.* n. 101
29. *Ibid.* n. 102
30. *Ibid.* n. 104
31. *Ibid.* n. 114
32. *Ibid.* n. 116
33. *Ibid.* n. 119
34. *Ibid.* n. 125
35. *Ibid.* n. 151
36. *Ibid.* n. 53